GW00542472

MANAGING INFORMATION

CIPD REVISION GUIDE 2005

David Allen is the CIPD's Associate Examiner for Managing Information.

Wendy McKenzie founded McKenzie Training Associates, a financial training consultancy, more than 20 years ago. Since then she has acquired an international reputation as a financial trainer, working with a range of organisations to develop business-focused financial training programmes.

Gerry Thomson has over 20 years' experience in the training and development field and has worked both as an independent management consultant and as an academic at the International Business School, Isle of Man.

The Chartered Institute of Personnel and Development is the leading publisher of books and reports for personnel and training professionals, students, and all those concerned with the effective management and development of people at work. For details of all our titles, please contact the publishing department:

tel: 020 8263 3387

fax: 020 8263 3850

e-mail: publish@cipd.co.uk

The catalogue of all CIPD titles can be viewed on the CIPD website:

www.cipd.co.uk/bookstore

MANAGING INFORMATION

CIPD REVISION GUIDE 2005

DAVID ALLEN
WENDY MCKENZIE
GERRY THOMSON

Chartered Institute of Personnel and Development

Published by the Chartered Institute of Personnel and Development,
CIPD House, Camp Road, London, SW19 4UX

First published 2005

© Chartered Institute of Personnel and Development, 2005

All rights reserved. No part of this publication may be reproduced, stored
in a retrieval system, or transmitted, in any form or by any means,
electronic, mechanical, photocopying, recording, or otherwise, without
the prior written permission of the publisher.
    This publication may not be sold, lent, hired out or otherwise dealt with
in the course of trade or supplied in any form of binding or cover other
than that in which it is published without the prior written permission of
the publisher.
    The rights of David Allen, Wendy McKenzie and Gerry Thomson to be
identified as authors of this work have been asserted by them in accordance
with sections 77 and 78 of the Copyright, Designs and Patents Act 1988.
    No responsibility for loss occasioned to any person acting or refraining
from action as a result of any material in this publication can be accepted
by the editor, author or publisher.

Design and typesetting by Curran Publishing Services, Norwich
Printed in Great Britain by The Cromwell Press, Trowbridge, Wiltshire

British Library Cataloguing in Publication Data
A catalogue record of this revision guide is available from the
British Library

ISBN 1 84398 094 0

The views expressed in this revision guide are the authors' own and may
not necessarily reflect those of the CIPD.
    The CIPD has made every effort to trace and acknowledge copyright
holders. If any source has been overlooked, CIPD Enterprises would be
pleased to redress this for future editions.

Chartered Institute of Personnel and Development, CIPD House,
Camp Road, London, SW19 4UX
Tel: 020 8971 9000   Fax: 020 8263 3333
Email: cipd@cipd.co.uk   Website: www.cipd.co.uk
Incorporated by Royal Charter. Registered Charity No. 1079797

CONTENTS

FIGURES

TABLES

PREFACE

Effective problem-solving and decision-making are the keys to the successful management of organisations. Both of these activities depend, to a very large extent, on competent information management.

With the developments of recent years in information technology, notably communications and computing hardware and software, sophisticated information management has become accessible to even the smallest of organisations. We have also seen the use of information technology (IT) spreading to all functions. Once used only in operational research departments and for payroll, its application is widespread in accounting, production planning, personnel, marketing and logistics.

The Managing Information module is designed to provide you with a basic and broad understanding of the role and function of information in the problem-solving, decision-making and communication processes of organisations.

The perspective adopted and explicit in the design of this module is thus that of an information/decision-making model of organisation. The techniques and methods of statistics and finance, which make up the remaining part of the module, can then be viewed as devices for transforming data into information for managerial problem-solving and decision-making.

In line with this perspective, the emphasis is not on the calculative aspects of the techniques, but on how the interpretation of the results received can inform and support managerial decision-making. Virtually no calculations will be required of you. However, we envisage that exceptionally you may want to carry out some elementary calculations in support of an argument or case. Questions will, therefore, focus more or less exclusively on the correct identification of the approach or principles to be used in a specific situation or problem and on the interpretation of the results of financial or statistical computations that will be given to you in the questions.

To turn to the module itself; the first section deals with the contribution made by information in the development of competitive effectiveness, thus providing the strategic context. This is much more to do with the creative use of information technology than with its use to reduce the amount of repetitive administrative and clerical work carried out manually by people. In the twenty-first century, managing information is about increasing competitive advantage through enhanced problem-solving, decision-making and communication within organisations. There are two broad dimensions to this. Internally, it means using IT to improve, for example, organisational learning and the transfer of knowledge and information between organisation members. Externally, it involves using IT to develop, for example, effective customer–supplier relationships and to create new distribution mechanisms for products and services. You need to familiarise yourself with the ways in which your organisation – or others that you may know about through wider reading – uses IT in its various functions.

A range of decision-making models is also introduced to you in this section. The expectation is that you will discuss, for example, the rational, limited rationality, disorder/garbage-can, symbolic, conflict and logical incrementalist models. Most importantly, you should understand the limitations of the rational approach, the concept of risk and the consequent difficulties for information system design. These difficulties are, of course, most apparent for information systems that support strategic-level decision-making. You will also need to be aware of the differences in the nature of the information and the time orientation of information systems at the different levels of an organisation.

Because the module is grounded in systems thinking, you need to understand the basic concepts of systems, so that you can develop knowledge of methodologies for the analysis and design of information systems. You should therefore be familiar with the basic tenets of general systems theory, and have an understanding of holism, emergence and complexity, together with the vocabulary of systems thinking.

For understanding the analysis and design of information systems at a more detailed level, you must be able to construct systems diagrams – that is, system maps, influence diagrams, multiple-cause diagrams and the range of data-flow diagrams. This will enable you to understand and carry out the basic data analysis and data-flow modelling which form part of information system design methodologies, such as the Structured Systems Analysis and Design

Methodology (SSADM). You must also know and understand database structures so that you can use database applications. These, together with spreadsheet modelling, enable you to understand the generation and input of reports to the managerial decision processes of your organisation.

The second section, Managing finance, is designed to provide you with a basic understanding of the role and function of financial and accounting information in the problem-solving, decision-making and communication processes of organisations. The techniques and methods of accounting are viewed as devices for transforming financial and accounting data into information for managerial problem-solving and decision-making.

Organisational performance at all levels is ultimately measured in financial terms, and many, if not most, important organisational decisions are based on financial criteria. As a personnel and development specialist, you need to understand the financial implications of your own decisions, those of your organisation generally, and those of any courses of action you might recommend. You therefore need to have a good working knowledge and understanding of the principles of finance and accounting.

To complete this part of the module successfully, you need to be familiar with the structure and elements of the main financial statements as enumerated in the standards, and the measures of performance, that is, ratios that can be obtained from these. The evaluation of projects or courses of action that you might recommend necessitates an understanding of appraisal techniques such as net present value (NPV), discounted cash flow (DCF) and cost–benefit analysis. Knowledge of budgetary planning and control, and the concepts and techniques that enable this type of system to be set up, is needed for making decisions on effectiveness of resource use.

As a personnel manager, you also need to be able to outline in financial terms any proposals that you intend to initiate, so that in enlisting the aid of an accountant to work out the details you can provide an adequate briefing. The quality of the financial presentation of any proposal is likely to determine the likelihood of its acceptance, in the face of competition for scarce resources from elsewhere in the organisation.

The third section of the module is intended to provide you with knowledge of the sources of data, internal and external to the organisation, and a basic understanding of statistical techniques, such as correlation, regression, time series analysis, significance testing and others as indicated in the standards. This will enable you to see how complex data can be analysed, interpreted and used to support organisation decision-making. It should also enable you to have meaningful discussions with specialists when commissioning surveys or having any kind of statistical analysis carried out. You should also develop competence in the use of spreadsheet packages such as Excel, to analyse data and present them in appropriate graphical formats.

To sum up: we see information systems as crucial processes in support of the planning, allocation and control of the organisation's resources and the attainment of competitive advantage.

It is important to note that this guide is intended to be read in conjunction with the recommended CIPD texts for this module – *Managing information and statistics* by Roland and Francis Bee and *Managing financial information* by David Davies. As such it is designed to guide you through the revision and examination process.

In Chapter 1 you are given a summary of the key contents of the module as indicated by the standards, together with suggestions as to the types of question that you might encounter. This will give you a good idea of the relationship between typical organisational problems, as encapsulated in questions, and the knowledge base that you should have acquired.

Chapter 2 offers advice on different ways of revision and how to manage effectively the time you have available for revision. Most importantly, it clarifies what is meant by analysis and evaluation, and shows you how to set out implementation plans.

Chapter 3 is intended to give you an insight into what the examiners expect, and the features of good and poor performance.

Finally, in Chapter 4 you are provided with worked examples of typical examination questions, with advice on how to 'deconstruct' them, so as to focus directly on what is required and what pitfalls to avoid.

SECTION 1

CIPD PROFESSIONAL STANDARDS

1 CIPD PROFESSIONAL STANDARDS

Introduction

It would not be unreasonable to say that information provides the lifeblood of the modern organisation. It flows through every facet, providing energy, generating ideas, guiding direction and effort and indicating the organisation's health. Information is essential to managerial decision-making, which is generally regarded as the heart of the organisation. In many respects the HR professional 'takes the organisation's temperature', assessing, advising and recommending courses of treatment to ensure its continued health. The prescription is simple – understanding information, its nuances, its reliability, its limitations, and its consistency.

This chapter provides you with a Managing Information Standards 'health check', helping you to focus on the essentials for understanding, analysing and interpreting the systems of a healthy organisation.

At the outset the Managing Information Standard set outs to provide a holistic approach to understanding the role and function of information in the decision-making and communication processes of the organisation. In the light of that approach, the skill you need is in the interpretation of financial and statistical information, rather than in mere number-crunching. Today's HR professional has to recognise the validity of using tools and techniques to counteract the intransigence of the business environment, while maintaining control of the information provided and the solutions generated. Unfortunately, many HR professionals are not good at using these tools and consequently fail to utilise the opportunities afforded by these techniques to enhance the quality of their decision-making.

The standards unravelled

Each of the CIPD's Professional Standards is divided into 'performance indicators', which in turn separate into distinct 'operational indicators' – things you are expected to be able to do – and 'knowledge indicators' – the concepts you should understand and be able to explain if necessary within the examination. The examination covers the spread of these indicators through a combination of Section A and Section B questions.

The second part of the CIPD's Professional Standard, the 'indicative content', is far more useful to know about as background for the examination, because it encompasses the width of the syllabus, listing in detail all the areas that your studies should focus on.

You must also remember that because of the holistic and integrative nature of the Standards, it is essential to demonstrate your understanding of Managing Information in the context of organisational situations, which by their very nature are dynamic and changing, and which interrelate with other parts of the organisation and its environment. This means that you ought to have a sound understanding of your business environment and your organisation in particular.

Understanding where finance fits in the HR role and the Professional Development Scheme

The CIPD sees the personnel or HR professional as a 'business partner' who is a 'thinking performer'. What do these terms mean? A 'business partner' is someone who can deliver day-to-day results while still being capable of contributing to personal, functional and corporate improvement. The 'thinking performer' contributes to the achievement and development of the organisation's broader strategic goals and objectives.

Three of the 10 core competencies can be assessed on the finance paper:

- business understanding
- analytical and intuitive/creative behaviour
- persuasion (part of persuasion and interpersonal skills).

And in the exam, you will need to show evidence of all of the five BACKUP skills:

- **b**usiness orientation

- **a**pplication **c**apability

- **k**nowledge of the subject

- **u**nderstanding

- **p**ersuasion and presentation skills.

To understand what the examiners are looking for you also need to remember two other things:

- This is a *postgraduate qualification*, which means that it is not good enough to regurgitate facts – you have to show that you understand the subject and the commercial consequences of decisions and options.

- The standard is clear – the questions will largely focus on the *interpretation* of statistics or financial statements.

Now you know what the examiners are measuring, let us look at how you can demonstrate your skills.

- It is crucial you understand what you are doing, as you are unlikely to have to perform any calculations, you need only offer explanations.

- Show the examiner what you know by giving detailed answers, but show your understanding by giving pros and cons and illustrating with relevant examples.

- Think outside of the box! It may sound heretical, but finance is not always the most important aspect in management decision-making. Every organisation has its 'loss leaders', for strategic reasons or to retain customer satisfaction. So if the question involves decision-making do not be afraid of introducing any non-financial factors that should be taken into account, as this illustrates your business orientation.

Present your information in a clear and concise way. You have a time constraint, so use diagrams, flow charts and so on to illustrate your points. Do not forget that the exam is also testing your persuasion and presentation skills.

Performance indicators

Operational indicators

The nine operational indicators here provide guidance to the areas in which you ought to be developing competence at work. You may well look at these indicators and say that you have little experience or opportunity to use them within a working context. On reflection, however, you ought to be able to see where you can practise these at work, incorporating them into your everyday tasks. This is essential as you begin to refocus your mind to thinking outside the 'personnel' box and tuning in to managing information better. By identifying opportunities where you can use simple information systems – for example, in setting up a simple process for handling complaints or providing a template for training a routine task – you will begin to think about information systems in a different way. This will also enable you to think about the nature of the data you will be providing within the organisation to satisfy its systems and software.

You have probably come across a situation in which you have found it difficult to 'interrogate' software, and most likely you have become frustrated at not being able to get the information that you wanted. By thinking about information and how it is structured, you will be in a stronger position to interact with information management professionals within your organisation to make sure that your information needs are better served.

Much of our time in the modern office environment is spent using software packages. We have developed a dependency. It is therefore no surprise to find that the operational indicators reflect this by focusing your attention on processing data, generating reports, and using communication and network software more effectively. This extends the role of the HR professional, enabling him or her to make a more constructive and positive contribution to the strategic direction of the organisation.

The emphasis for HR professionals has changed. Expectations of the levels of skills and abilities required have risen to a new height. In essence, that means that the HR professional now has to develop more analysis and interpretation skills than previously. And that is why the operational indicators stress the need for interpreting statistical information and financial statements. As organisations need more often and more scrupulously to assess the contribution of staff, compare their performance through benchmarking and detect any undercurrents that are likely to hinder or interfere with progress, the HR professional is required to develop his or her ability to search for and collect data to serve all these purposes.

Because each and every activity undertaken within the organisation has implications on profit contribution, it is essential for HR professionals to be numerate and to be able to calculate expenditure, and understand costings and the implications of budgets. Through monitoring and careful control, these activities may be managed effectively and efficiently in keeping with the organisation's traditions.

Knowledge indicators

It is here – coupled with the indicative content – that you are likely to see everything you reckon to know in your work reflected in the examination. But it would be unwise to try to match each of the questions to any single knowledge indicator, because by the integrative nature of managing information the questions are unlikely to be completely discrete. When looking beforehand at the knowledge you are expected to develop through your studies, you will need to match these 11 indicators with the more specific indicative content. Table 1 will help you with this. It also maps the relevant chapters from the set texts.

Table 1 The Managing Information standard analysed

	Knowledge indicator		Indicative content	Recommended reading
1	The strategic role of information systems (IS), information technology (IT) and communication	Intro1	The contribution of IS/IT to the attainment of competitive advantage/ competitive effectiveness by organisations	Roland and Frances Bee: *Managing information and statistics* Chapters 1, 8

2	Organisational decision-making process	**Intro2**	Decision-making processes in organisations – eg rational, limited rationality, disorder, conflict, symbolic, and emergent – and the role of information, risk and sensitivity analysis	Bee Chapters 1, 2
3	The basic communication process	**Intro3**	Communication processes; interpretation and filtering out of information	Bee Chapters 3, 18
		Stats1	Presentation of statistics; sources of data	
4	Systems concepts	**Syst1**	Systems concepts: definition of a system, structure and process, holism, emergent properties	Bee Chapter 2
		Syst2	Systems attributes: boundary, environment, open, closed, lag, positive and negative feedback control model	Chapters 2, 3, 4
5	Elementary database concepts	**Syst3**	Data analysis: entities, attributes and relationships; systems and data-flow diagrams; data models – file management systems, hierarchical, network and relationship databases	Bee Chapters 5, 6

		Syst6	Current software applications for data processing, report generation, modelling and communication	Chapters 3, 5, 8
6	The range and nature of organisational information systems	**Syst**4	The organisation from an information perspective – eg types of organisation information systems, informational requirements of different organisational functions and activities	Bee Chapters 1, 7
7	Systems design methodology	**Syst**5	Methodologies for systems analysis and design – eg Structured Systems Analysis and Design Method (SSADM)	Bee Chapter 6
		Syst6	Current software applications for data processing, report generation, modelling and communication	Chapters 3, 5, 8
8	The financial statements and the flow of money in a business	**Acc**1	Structure and interpretation of simple balance sheets, profit and loss accounts, trading statements	David Davies: *Managing financial information*
		Acc2	Calculation and interpretation of management ratios	
		Acc3	Basic costing concepts and techniques; standard costing; budgets; cost benefit analysis; costing cash budgets; introduction	

			to discounted cash flows and project appraisal	
9	Basic statistical concepts	**Stats**1	Presentation of statistics; sources of data	Bee Chapters 9,10,11, 17
		Stats2	Statistical concepts: frequency distributions; mean; standard deviation; index numbers; significant tests; correlation and regression; times series analysis; control charts	Bee Chapters 9, 11, 17, 12–16
		Stats3	Use of current software application for computation of statistics; simple business calculations	Chapters 9–19
10	The implications for management of data protection legislation	**Intro**4	Data protection legislation; data security	Bee Chapter 1
11	Contingency planning for disaster recovery	**Intro**2	Decision-making processes in organisa- tions – eg rational, limited rationality, disorder, conflict, symbolic, and emer- gent – and the role of information, risk and sensitivity analysis	Bee Chapter 1
		Acc3	Basic costing concepts and techniques; stan- dard costing; budgets; cost benefit analysis; costing cash budgets; introduction to discounted cash flows and project appraisal	Davies

As is evident from the table, there is quite a large amount of content to absorb. The emphasis is on using the information for good decision-making, with a small amount of calculations. That does not mean that the arithmetical aspect of the course may be neglected. Far from it. You will need a working knowledge of statistical techniques because they will enhance your understanding and appreciation of other people's views. Similarly, being able to identify the right information required to calculate management ratios gives you a better appreciation of what actually is happening within the organisation. It also enables an HR professional to talk in the same language as his or her financial colleagues, and provides a more solid base from which you can influence the strategic managerial decision-making process within your organisation.

Indicative content

The Standards split the indicative content into four distinct areas:

- introduction

- systems

- accounting and finance

- statistics.

This separates each area into its constituent parts. You may astutely have spotted, however, that both the accounting and finance and the statistics are essentially subsystems, and contribute to the overall information system of the organisation.

Introduction content

The first area comprises an Introduction that provides an overview of information systems (IS) and information technology (IT), relating them to an organisation's competitive stance and need for efficiency and effectiveness of operation. Today's markets are intensely competitive, and the organisations that operate within them require a range and depth of information about:

- their own capabilities

- the needs and behaviours of their customers and clients

- the capability and competence of their competitors

- the rapidly changing external environment.

The organisation's information systems and information technology must reflect this range and harness the potential of that information to gain insight and reduce the risks in decision-making. Much of this is done through the filtering and interpretation of information and by maintaining security over it.

What do I really need to know?

Within the introductory section you will be expected to have a broad understanding of managing information. This means that you should be familiar with:

- how information is used in your organisation and in other organisations: for example, routine reports, exception reports, request reports and special reports (core text p9)

- what factors impact on information systems: for example, political, economic, social, technological, legal and educational

- how information can aid decision-making and maintain competitive advantage: for example, forecasting, planning, reviewing and controlling

- what the current trends are: for example, use of the Internet, decision support systems, the virtual reality organisation

- how information systems/information technology/trends might impact on HR, for example, increase training, create new ways of working, make people redundant.

Your knowledge here will be gained through your additional study, reading professional magazines – *People Management*, searching the CIPD website, reading the quality press – *The Times,* the *Guardian,* the *Telegraph* and the *Independent.* A good starting point to refresh your memory might be to re-read Chapter 1, pages 3 to 22, and Chapter 8, pages 97 to 103, of the core text, *Managing information and statistics* by Roland and Frances Bee.

In the exam, questions tend to be part of another one usually in Section B. A good example is Question 8 in the May 2003 paper.

> You have been asked to give a talk to the local CIPD branch on the ways that Information Systems/IT can help organisations achieve their goals and meet future challenges. Identify the key points you would make in your talk, and illustrate them with examples from your organisation.

Again Question 3 in May 2004 illustrates this well:

> Review the ways in which Information Technology might help to change management practices in your organisation, drawing on your knowledge of the latest developments in IT applications.

Systems content

The second area focuses primarily on the need for systems. Part 1 of the set text, *Managing information and statistics* by Roland and Frances Bee, covers this area very well. The section is almost an 'everything you always wanted to know about systems but were afraid to ask'. It will not turn you instantly into a systems analyst, but it will provide you with sufficient information to be able to understand what the information systems specialist is talking about. It will provide you with the jargon and language.

Information systems can by themselves constitute a complete business in their own right, so in relation to them a manager must be concerned with the normal organisational and managerial issues – location, control and operation. Systems must not only provide business support but also enable the organisation to transform its business methodologies to meet the demands of its business goals. In the light of this, the HR professional must possess a comprehensive understanding of the impact made by the systems, of the parts that contribute to a continually successful whole, and of the areas that require redesign to facilitate the achievement of HR's and the organisation's strategy.

This begins with an examination of a system and how it works, and goes on by looking at the constituent parts of database systems that provide a service orientation, and at other technologies that assist with the decision-making process, thereby influencing rather than controlling the business. The sophistication of modern work environments demands increasingly complex approaches to information systems resources – but not at the expense of effective backbone services. The HR professional as a direct service user can therefore comment constructively.

The idea that information systems are decision-support-oriented structures was put forward in the early 1980s by IBM, and has led to user-controlled computing. This whole approach ought to direct our thinking towards acknowledging the importance of a systems environment, towards stressing the interrelationship between all the different sections and parts of the organisation, and towards underlining the basic principles of cause and effect and their relationship to the decision-making process.

What do I really need to know?

This section is perhaps the crux of the topic and covers the essential knowledge you must have about systems:

- how they work

- how they are used by management, for planning, for control

- how they are designed

- how they can be applied for decision-making, to HR.

The bulk of your knowledge will come from Bee and will follow through Chapters 2–7. In addition you may supplement your knowledge and understanding by reading more widely on the subject. (Bee provides you with some additional reading texts on page 271. You can also find many in you local college/study centre library, direct from the British Library through interlibrary loan, or from the CIPD library.)

In the exam, you will find both Section A questions and Section B questions on this topic. This gives a clear indication of the importance of this part of the syllabus.

For example, in May 2003 these included Section A Question 1, the Childminders plc mini case and Section B Question 1 (both printed below).

Section A, Question I

You have been hired as an *information systems consultant* to Childminders plc, a chain of five-day care for infants, toddlers and pre-school age children in South East England.

Joan Smithson began the company 10 years ago when she expanded a small, *informal pre-school group* at her home into Childminders' first full-service centre.

Since that time Joan has added *four additional centres* to the company and during the next five years she expects to *double the size* of the company by opening five more. She caters mainly for the *day care of children* of professional couples, but also has *several contracts* with *local organisations* to provide crèches for their workforce *and* with *social services* to provide a day nursery service for infants in temporary foster care.

Each service centre has approximately *60 children* and has *12 to 15 staff members*. Until now Joan has used a combination of part-time clerical employees to meet the administration needs of the company and outside services to provide the payroll. Most of the administration is still *dependent* on a *manual system*, although there are *computers at* the five *centres* for clerical purposes and basic accounts.

At the moment, Joan is able to exercise a *reasonable* level of *managerial control* over most aspects of the business, through frequent visits to the five centres and close communication with her managers. She realises however, that with the additional centres this is going to be more difficult, particularly since the *planning* and start-up phases of each new project are likely to be very time-consuming. She is therefore looking to *introduce* a *new information system* to support her management of the business.

Joan has a reasonably clear idea of what she would like the new system to achieve. She wants the managers to have *effective systems* for:

- enrolment of infants
- attendances
- payment of fees
- maintenance of the building and contents
- purchase of new equipment

- staff records, including the important background search results, attendance, absence, training
- health and safety records
- budgeting.

For herself, she would like to be provided with an *overview* of what is going on in the centres, general social trends, legislative developments affecting childcare and an aid for making decisions on possible improvements.

Write a *report* for Joan Smithson *identifying the key decision areas* for her and her managers, and *specify the system* that will *support decision-making* in these areas. You should make use of appropriate diagrams in your report and justify the choice of systems.

Section B, Question 1

You are at a management meeting discussing the possible use of Information Technology (IT) consultants to review and redesign information systems in your organisation. Your colleagues want to know how the consultants might approach this task. What would you tell them? Justify your answer.

In the May 2004 exam (you can download the paper from the CIPD site), again Section A Question 1 (the compulsory question) and Section B Questions 1, 3 and 4 drew from this section of the syllabus.

Accounting and finance content

What is the standard's purpose?

Accounting and finance is part of the core management standard, which aims to 'provide a holistic understanding of the role and function of information in the decision and communication processes of organisations'. This means that its objective is to integrate accounting and statistics into an information, or decision-making, model of an organisation. Consequently it views accounting as a way of transforming data into information that can be used for:

- setting objectives

- measuring the effectiveness of resource use within budgetary systems

- managerial decision-making.

This means that in the exam you are:

- unlikely to have to perform any financial calculations
- expected to be able to interpret financial information, and use it effectively in decision-making.

Why am I studying finance?

When you are preparing for an exam, it is worth considering what the exam is testing. The CIPD believes that a modern HR professional is someone who can:

- deliver day-to-day results while still being capable of contributing to personal, functional, and corporate improvement
- contribute to the achievement and development of the organisation's broader strategic goals and objectives.

This means that you have to be able to:

✓ interpret basic trading accounts and balance sheets

✓ decide on financial performance standards, cost standards and cash budgets

✓ calculate expenditure on work programmes

✓ monitor and control income and expenditure against budgets.

The third area concerns accounting and finance. The concepts are very adequately covered in the set text, *Managing financial information* by David Davies. Once again the emphasis is on understanding and interpreting a range of financial data. As an HR professional you ought to be familiar with simple balance sheets, trading statements and profit and loss accounts, and be able to interpret the information presented. These documents are essential to understanding the 'money-go-round' and form the basis on which every business functions. Management ratios provide a snapshot of the health of a business, and you must become familiar with them and be at ease in both calculating and interpreting their meaning. Lastly, the whole budgeting and costing process must be understood in order for you to financially manage the

HR area effectively. That means knowing the difference between marginal and absorption costing, and the effect the use of either of these can have on profit. In addition, a sound knowledge of budgeting and financial control will ensure that your targets are met and that the service levels you provide for other parts of the organisation remain effective. Cost–benefit analysis and discounted cash flow are both tools that assist in decision-making, enabling you to argue more successfully for resources and demonstrating that you are aware of all the implications of your requests.

What am I expected to know?

There are three broad financial subject areas covered by the standard.

First, you are expected to understand and be able to interpret *financial statements*. This covers simple balance sheets, trading statements, and profit and loss accounts.

The second subject area is largely concerned with interpretation of financial statements, as you are expected to be able to both calculate and interpret *management ratios*. These ratios are interrelated, but can be broadly classified into solvency, profitability and efficiency ratios. (Chapters 7, 8 and 13.)

The third subject area is *management accounting*. You are expected to both understand and be able to use:

- costing concepts and techniques including absorption costing (sometimes called full costing) and marginal costing (Chapters 9–12.)

- standard costing (Chapters 9–12.)

- cash flow (Chapters 4–6.)

- the principles of planning and budgeting (including the preparation of cash budgets) (Chapters 14–16.)

- project appraisal techniques including payback, accounting rate of return, cost benefit analysis, and discounted cash flow (particularly present value and net present value). (Chapter 16.)

The emphasis is on interpretation and use, rather than calculation. Key chapters are 2, 3, 6, 7, and 16 as they have particular relevance for personnel specialists and information systems. These chapters will provide you with some background knowledge and how it is applied in context.

Thinking about the standard and preparing for the examination

The most important thing to remember is that you are an HR professional, not an accountant!

Unfortunately the language used at the top of organisations is primarily financial. As a contributing HR professional you have to understand it, and be able to use financial information in your decision-making. This is what the exam will be testing, and so you have to understand as much about the 'why' as the 'what'. You have to understand the subject well enough to be able to discuss the pros and cons of using a particular technique, or ratio, in a specific situation.

In the exam you will find financial questions in both Sections A and B. In Section A they can relate to costing (as in May 2003):

> Your organisation has three main products and a report has just been produced by the accountants on product line three. A senior management meeting is to be held shortly to discuss the future of line three and your manager would like you to explain the financial information in the report. He has left the following two tables on your desk.

Table 1

Product Line	1	2	3	Total
Budgeted sales (units)	20000	8000	12000	
	£000	£000	£000	£000
Sales revenue	600	400	300	1300
Direct materials	200	80	120	400
Direct labour	100	140	160	400
Production overhead	150	60	70	280
Non-production overhead	30	20	10	60
	480	300	360	1140
Profit(Loss)	120	100	(60)	160

Table 2

Product Line	1	2	3	Total
Budgeted sales(units)	20000	8000	12000	
	£000	£000	£000	£000
Sales revenue	600	400	300	1300
Less variable costs:				
Direct materials	200	80	120	400
Direct labour	100	140	160	400
Variable production overhead	20	28	32	80
	320	248	312	880
Contribution	280	152	(12)	420
Less fixed costs				(200)
Non-production overheads				(60)
Profit				160

N.B.

1. The total production overhead of £280,000 consists of £80,000 variable costs and £200,000 fixed costs. Variable production overheads are absorbed on the basis of 20% of the direct labour costs.

2. The non-production overhead of £60,000 is fixed.

Write a report for your manager, with reference to the above tables, explaining the difference between absorption and marginal costing. Discuss the effect the different approaches might have on what decision was taken.

Alternatively the questions can relate to capital budgeting, as in May 2004 (you can download this paper from the CIPD website).

Section B questions are often more inquisitive, and test your specific knowledge within the areas. Examples from May 2003 are given below. In May 2004 they were Questions 2, 5 and 10.

Question 2

Your manager has put forward a project to be considered for the capital budget next year, and has been informed by the finance director that the Net Present Value method will be used to appraise all projects. Your manager has asked for a brief explanation of this approach, and for comments on the strengths and weaknesses of this approach compared to any other method.

Question 3

The Chief Executive Officer has asked you to outline a good practice budgetary planning and control template for him so that he can identify the parts of the process that need attention in your organisation.

Question 5

You have been asked to give a short talk to supervisors on interpreting your organisation's accounts using ratio analysis. Outline the key points, and justify your choice.

As you can see from the format above you can get up to four questions in the finance area, one covering each of the main topics. If finance is your strong point, a solid understanding will provide you with a confident base from which to pass the exam.

Statistical content

The last area focuses on the tools and techniques of statistics. These are to be found in Part 2 of *Managing information and statistics* by Roland and Frances Bee. It is perhaps the area that evokes most concern among students – although that concern is often ill-founded and stems back to poor teaching throughout schooling.

The techniques you will explore are valuable, and should easily be incorporated into your everyday life at work. The tip is to utilise them frequently so that their use becomes automatic. Often we do not think in statistical terms about many of the activities we do at work – they are jobs that just have to be done. For many people such an attitude might seem commendable in that as soon as they think in statistical terms, the barriers come down and they end up with a mental block. You cannot afford to have that be what happens in your case.

The process of gathering information is difficult, yet the more information collected, the greater the likelihood that the decision made will be correct. To ensure this, it is necessary to organise your information to prevent confusion, and to separate the relevant information from the irrelevant. By treating information in this way you are more likely to be able to measure objectives, justify your actions and demonstrate effectiveness. Think about it. When presented with facts, very few managers challenge the assumptions made, and a great number of decisions seem to be taken on the basis of a 'fait accompli'. By studying this section you will improve your powers of persuasion and produce better decisions.

Statistical techniques are naturally used in other parts of the course, particularly for benchmarking, or to survey staff attitudes, or to compare the trends in reward and benefit packages. In essence, we are surrounded by statistical information, so the good HR professional is careful to use the tools to his or her best advantage. The concepts are really the nitty-gritty of calculation, and can often be tiresome. You need to know what the answers to the calculations tell you, rather than be entrenched in working out the computations. It is better to know what a time series tells you, or what relevance standard deviation has for recruitment and selection, than to know how to work them out. Bear in mind that the examination is only two hours long, including 10 minutes' reading. In most cases that would not allow you the time to do every single one of the calculations following the techniques you will have studied. You should also bear in mind that the presentation of statistical information plays a major part in report writing, providing feedback on performance, predicting events and forecasting trends, and is therefore integral to the work of the HR professional.

What do I need to know?

This is perhaps the most difficult area to study for, because the concepts are so wide and varied. To help you, it is best to try and group the topics under broader headings. I suggest the following:

- General communication (Chapters 9–11, 19).

- Probability, sampling (Chapters 12–14).

- Planning and decision-making (Chapters 15–18).

By looking at the syllabus in this way, you are preparing yourself for the broad questions that can arise in the examination. As with the previous section, you are likely to get examination questions in both Sections A and B. For example, in May 2003 this question was set:

Question 3

Your manager has been grappling with the issue of workforce requirements for next year and has been trying to make predictions. She has given the company statistician the data below, showing sales per quarter for the past five years, from which, using the assumed annual sales turnover per employee (£200,000), the workforce requirements for the next two years can be calculated.

SALES FIGURES (£M)

Quarter		1	2	3	4
Year	1999	52.3	55.4	53.7	50.6
	2000	54.2	55.5	54.9	53.4
	2001	55.1	56.6	55.2	54.3
	2002	56.3	59.2	57.5	55.4

The company statistician has produced a report for your manager, and she has left you a note asking for an explanation of the following highlighted items on the report she has received from him.

Seasonal factors:	Quarter 1	0.998
	Quarter 2	1.034
	Quarter 3	1.004
	Quarter 4	0.964

Trend equation is $T = 52.58 + 0.28t$ (where t is the time period expressed in quarters)

A multiplicative model has been used.

Write a report for your manager explaining these figures and commenting on other factors you need to take into account in making any predictions. Discuss the degree of caution you should adopt in using these predictions.

This question draws from the planning and decision-making area, whereas in the May 2004 paper the question drew from the probability and sampling area. It is likely that these two sections will provide the bulk of the Section A questions.

In May 2003, Section B questions drew from all three sections and focused on decision-making, sampling and index numbers.

Question 4

You are discussing your proposal for training junior managers in decision-making. One of the senior line managers queries the spending on this, saying, 'Decision-making skill is to do with experience and intuition.' Explain whether or not this is a balanced view.

Question 6

You have received the following e-mail from your manager: 'I've just been reading about comparing survey results year on year, and the article talks about goodness of fit tests. What does this mean?'

Question 9

A colleague in the human resources team suggests that some people management and development data should be kept in index number form. Explain, discuss and illustrate this idea.

Question 10

During an informal chat over coffee, one of your colleagues questions the usefulness of management theories. Explain to your sceptical colleague what insights into decision-making can be gained by drawing on decision analysis/theory.

In May 2004, Question 7 tackled sampling, and Questions 8 and 9 concerned general communication (these can be downloaded from the CIPD website).

Conclusion

Throughout this short chapter I have tried to summarise and talk you through the some of the thinking associated with the Managing Information Professional Standards and the examination. You will have recognised that the emphasis is on understanding and how information can be an asset to management. Computations will be minimal, although developing your knowledge in this area will benefit your understanding. The next chapter is intended to give examination candidates a more specific insight into what the examiners have in mind by discussing the sort of questions they set, and the reasoning behind the way in which those questions are posed.

Many students try to outguess the examiner and spend an inordinate amount of time matching and cross-matching questions from previous years to try to predict the questions in the next exam. I personally try to avoid this, as sod's law will say what I have studied as certainty will be omitted that year by the examiner. By all means check previous exams, but look at broader headings. At present it is clear that Section A is broken into three questions, one on systems, one on finance and one on statistics. Section B is guaranteed to have questions on each of those areas. How many is determined by the examiner, but at least two will be on systems, three on financial aspects and three on statistics. Whether that balance may alter, we do not know: only the examiner does.

SECTION 2

HOW TO TACKLE REVISION
AND THE EXAMINATION

2 REVISION AND EXAMINATION GUIDANCE

Introduction

The hard part is over – you have completed the syllabus: all you need to do now is revise and sit the exam. Easy, isn't it? But this is an important time for you. And because it is, you must prepare meticulously to ensure your success. Always remember: if you feel confident, that feeling will permeate through your whole approach, even to the day of the exam.

Your preparation will focus on your revision and the exam. This chapter is devised to help your preparation in both areas.

Tackling revision

The key to success is *planning*.

Planning your time

You will have many decisions to make. The first concerns how much time you will have available for revising. It may well mean juggling your home, work and social life. Be clear. Allocate yourself a set amount of time and then manage your revision around that time. It need not mean that you use every spare minute of your day – remember that if you are tired, you will be less productive. Set aside time so that you can maximise the effective use of that time by planning your study.

One thing you will learn as you develop through your professional studies is that everyone is different. Yes – that means you too! You will need to determine what time best suits you. Are you a morning or an evening person? Has your organisation given you study time? Have you taken study time as holiday? Do you intend to work only in the evenings or at the weekends? Whatever pattern you decide, stick to it. This will certainly involve strong resolve and discipline, for you will undoubtedly be tempted to waiver and may be distracted.

It is a well-known fact that protracted periods of intense studying are unproductive. This means that you should build in breaks to re-energise your body and mind. Take five minutes off to have a drink or to do something completely different, such as reading the newspaper or listening to music. This should enable you to come back fresh. A time-out is particularly useful when you find yourself bogged down in a question and struggling to find an answer.

Stress is probably something that you have become more aware of lately, particularly in the lead-up to your exam. You ought to be able to recognise the symptoms and identify the causes. For the modern busy student there can be a number of problems when you are juggling work, family, social life and study. Stress can be positive or negative. We need some stress to generate adrenalin to give us feelings of elation, exhilaration and delight, yet more often than not our body over-reacts, causing anxiety, worry and increased despair. At this time of the year we need to identify a menu of coping techniques that will help us generate positiveness. These range from clarifying your beliefs and objectives, that is, what you want out of life and where you are heading, to relaxation techniques such as yoga, meditation and breathing exercises.

Take time out from this guide and explore another you.
Close your eyes.
Breath in slowly but deeply.
Breath out slow and long.
Concentrate on your body.
Think about relaxing each part in turn: your head, your neck, your shoulders, your arms, your back, your thighs your legs, your toes.
Breathe in deeply and slowly as you exhale. Feel the relaxation spreading to the very ends of your fingers and toes.
Take another deep breath. Slowly inhale, hold for a few seconds.
Breathe out slow and long.
Open your eyes.
Stretch your body gently.

(Adapted from a relaxation course attended some years ago)

Details of such activities can be found in many different places, such as magazines, the Internet, books on stress, and occupational health leaflets. They may appear silly, but they do set you up and put you in the right frame of mind to study productively. The power of positive thought is underestimated. Think positively and you will achieve; think negatively and you will increase the level of stress you find yourself under. As I have already said, stress is a combination of different factors: family, job, culture, organisation and self. You have to balance these factors to achieve equilibrium. The key to this is time management. Many organisations lay on courses in time management for their staff. If possible, try to attend one. The principles explained during the course can be applied equally to study and to work. If you cannot attend a course, the following may help and assist you.

Time management

Prioritising your time is key. This means clearly identifying how you use your time, and them classifying your time into four areas, using criteria such as important and urgent. A priority framework can be generated into which you can allocate all your activity (see Figure 1).

Urgent and important **Priority 1**	Important but non urgent **Priority 2**
Urgent but not important **Priority 3**	Non urgent and not important **Priority 4**

Figure 1 Time management

Watch out for time wasters. These include distractions, your own perfectionism, disorganisation and not having the relevant information to hand, intrusions, visitors, answering the telephone, conversations, and waiting or hanging around, say at the dentist, or for a bus or train. Many of these can be managed, and you need only to consider some of the following:

- Look at the layout of your study area. Does it manage you or do you manage it? Consider having a clear desk policy. That means having enough area for you to work in an uncluttered manner. It does not mean pushing everything out of sight. Clear up as you go. When finished with one text, put it away and move on to another. Try to make your breaks coincide with natural stoppages in your study.

- Work out a system for sorting your papers. The maxim is to handle every piece of paper once. This also means having an appropriate filing system with relevant sections covering the course syllabus.

- Writing and reading can be done with skill. Use note-taking, speed-reading, mind maps and other techniques mentioned previously. Summarise and record your revision.

- When choosing the most time-effective method of travel, take into account how much work can be done on the journey.

- Set time limits and stick to them. This could be for revising a topic or topic area, or for talking to friends and family. Get to the point quickly and avoid small talk. That way visitors and family members know how much time you can give them. Always have a clock visible so that you can see it. This makes you more conscious of time as it ticks away. Write down beginning and end times – this habit will stand you in good stead when you tackle the exam.

- Use call-back procedures for telephone calls. Ring back at a time that is more convenient for you. Leave messages, but keep them short and simple. In dealing with children and partners, ask for feedback to confirm their understanding of messages and instructions.

- Above all, set yourself clear objectives and you will find that you are managing you time more effectively and preparing well for your examinations.

Once you have determined how much time you have available, make sure it is quality time. That means informing other people in your household of your intentions. It also means switching off your mobile phone, putting the house phone on the answermachine, finding somewhere quiet where you can spread out, and beginning your studies in a conducive atmosphere.

What you are going to revise

You will need to allocate time to each of the topic areas of the syllabus. This might mean going back to the performance indicators and using these as a guideline – Table 1 (page 7) should help you. A good rule of thumb is to identify the topics you feel most comfortable with and allocate the least time to them. You can then allow more time for the areas that you have identified as weaker. Avoid concentrating too much effort in one area, because that might severely hamper your chances of success.

It is no good trying to revise without *objectives*. Identify what you want to achieve in each revision period. The objectives should be realistic and achievable. It would, for instance, take more than half an hour to complete the design and evaluation of a SSADM for your organisation, or to outline all the database design issues that are of concern to the HR function.

It is essential to stick to your plan. On the other hand you must have contingency measures for unexpected interruptions. Have you built in some slack time so that you can get back on schedule if you lose time through no fault of your own? You might have to work late; unexpected visitors might arrive; the washing machine might give up the ghost and cause major water damage. You have probably experienced problems like these when revising for previous examinations.

When you have completed sections of your plan, think about ways of keeping your motivation up. Perhaps reward yourself with a treat – a glass of wine or bar of chocolate, or watching a video. Tell your partner or friends how well you are doing, and get them to be pleased that you are pleased, which will encourage you further. If you have written your revision plan out as a schedule, highlight the parts of your plan that you have done, to indicate the progress you have made. Whatever you do, feel good about it – and build your confidence.

Structure your revision

The structure of your planned revision is important, and this is an area that many students struggle with. Few have had any guidance on how to study. Everyone is just expected to know how to do it, but no one can know without being told or shown, and many students fall down here. Within the People Management and Development area and the general and specialist electives, you will no doubt develop a number of your own approaches to learning. However, this revision guide suggests four tried and tested ways of approaching your revision:

- Write it down.
- Read it.
- Explain it.
- Just do it.

Write it down

Making copious notes throughout the year will give you a solid basis for your revision. These notes should be refined and revised. If you adopt this approach, make sure you have a folder to store your revision notes in or you will drown in a sea of paper.

Think about creative ways of writing down the key points. Use checklists or find lists of questions for you to answer. Try the questions identified in Chapter 1. If you are familiar with mind maps (see Figure 2), draw one for each of the performance indicators. Produce information cards that you can take with you to work, to look at on the train or bus or during lunch. These cards should be of a handy size, and enable you to avoid taking all your revision books and notes with you everywhere you go. Figures 3 and 4 are examples.

Read it

The more reflective among you have probably highlighted your text for reading later. A tip is not to highlight huge areas on the page, so that all that confronts you is one vast block of colour. It is best to highlight keywords or phrases only. These can then be used as the nub and tendrils of mind maps. The technique here is to read and reread until you are comfortable with the subject matter.

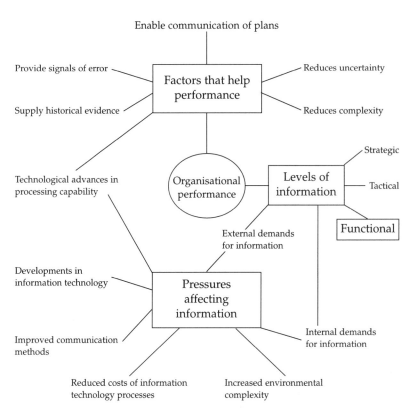

Figure 2 Mind map: information on organisational performance

Things to do – Try it for yourself
Download Question 1 Section A May 2003 (the mini case study on Childminders plc). Highlight the key words. When you have done this go back to Chapter 1 and look at the question as it is printed there. I have highlighted what I consider to be the key words. Compare your answer with mine. Your page should not be full of highlights, but the key words should stand out.

Overleaf is a mind map showing the key decision areas for this question.

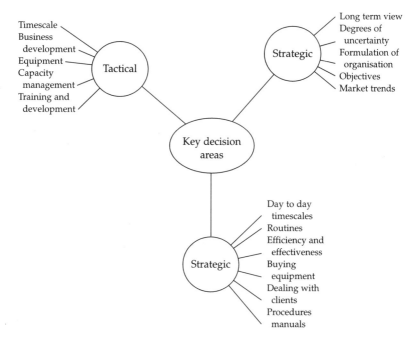

Figure 3 Sample mind map for Section A Question 1, May 2003

Explain it

This approach involves your explaining concepts to others. It is easiest to try if you have set up a study group. If you have not, try it out on a partner who can check whether or not you are correct from the relevant section in the book or from your notes. By tackling your revision in this way you will clarify any misunderstanding and tighten up on aspects you are unsure of. By verbalising the issues, you also begin to put together the kind of answer you are likely to have to come up with in the exam.

Here is one for you to try
Explain out loud or to your partner the main parts of SSADM.
Compare your answer with mine (given on page 38).

Ratio analysis
- provide more meaningful information
- help interpret data
- determine relationships between figures
- need to be interpreted in light of other information

Major ratios
- Measures of effectiveness
  - Gross Profit
  - Adminstrative %
  - ROI
- Measures of short term solvency
  - Current Ratio
  - Liquidity ratio
- Measures of performance of working capital management
  - Debtor days
  - Creditor days
  - Stockturnover

Reasons for poor GP ratio
- careless stock control
- defalcations of cash received from sales
- rising cost not passed on to customer
- change in the sales mix
- inaccurate stock inventory

Reasons for Low Current and Liquidity ratios
- delay payment of creditors
- problems finding weekly wage cash
- creditors withhold supplies due to late payment
- replacement of fixed assets postponed
- investment plans shelved or postponed.

Figure 4 Sample information card on ratio analysis

SSADM consists of three main components

- the default structure or framework of a SSADM project

- a set of standard analysis and design techniques

- the products of each techniques.

The structure of a SSADM is based on a number of modules:

- feasibility study

- requirements analysis

- requirement specification

- logical systems specification

- physical design.

SSADM looks at a system from three perspectives:

- the functionality or processing

- the data

- the effects of time and real world events.

Just do it

Perhaps the most frequently used approach by students is to do examination questions from previous papers. The technique here is simple. Allocate yourself 25 minutes for a Section A question or 10 minutes for a Section B question. Then answer the question set. Remember the total allocations of marks for Section A and Section B are identical, although more detail and explanation of concepts are expected in Section A's questions.

Submit your attempt to your tutor for marking. When you receive your returned script, pay attention to the comments made by your tutor. These should help point you in the right direction or highlight weak areas of your answer. Better tutors will also provide you with hints on how to be more concise in your answers.

Practise doing 30-second answer planning for Section B questions.

(See the November 2003 examination questions at the end of this chapter.)

Wherever possible, try to identify key topics

Key topics are often determined by what is happening in the business environment, and reported in the news and business press. The exam is always set six months in advance of your sitting, so go back six or so months as part of your research. Refer to the performance indicators – these are the key areas of competence and form the framework for the examination. In Chapter 1 the content is broken down into some key topics, check it out.

Above all, be confident

You have probably sat exams before. You certainly have been successful in previous examinations, and there is no reason to believe you will not be successful in these. Be calm. There is no need to panic. You will have prepared adequately by planning your revision, and you will therefore have all the knowledge necessary at your fingertips. Be assured – and follow the steps outlined in the section below to guarantee success.

Tackling the examination

Before the examination

- Relax. Get up in plenty of time.

- Have breakfast. This will be the most important meal you will have today. It is essential to feed the body to help activate your brain.

- Ensure that you have pens (which work), pencils, ruler, rubber, sharpener, calculator and spare batteries, 'concentration sweets', drink if necessary and/or allowed, lucky mascot, identification for invigilators, and any other essential documentation. It is best to construct a checklist in advance of all the things you will require on the day. Then all you need to do is tick them off. This gives you a positive start and begins the mental confidence process early.

- You should also have prepared your route to the examination venue. A good tip if you have never been there before is to take a trip out to locate the venue. Do this at the time you would expect to leave on the day of the examination. By pre-planning you are most likely to anticipate any difficulties or problems you are likely to incur on your journey.

- Listen to the local radio for any road works or delays, so that you can alter your route as necessary.

- On arrival, greet fellow students you know – but do not discuss your revision or questions with them. Find your own space to gather your thoughts. Discussion with others serves only serves to place questions in your mind about either the adequacy of your revision, or topics that you think you know very little about.

- Be positive. You have prepared. You are ready for the examination.

In the examination

The Managing Information examination follows a structure similar to that of all the other CIPD professional exams. You have to complete questions from Section A and questions from Section B. You are granted 10 minutes' reading time. This is important and should be used constructively.

- Read through the whole paper quickly. This gives you a feel for the exam.

- Then read the paper a second time. During this time, read with your pencil in your hand. Mark questions you feel able to answer, or write down the topic area being covered or points that spring to mind. At no time should you be trying to structure an answer at this stage.

- Your objective is to get a feel for the paper and to absorb the rubric (the instructions given at the beginning of the paper).

- A key part of the rubric for you is that *both sections of the examination carry equal marks*. For Section A this means that each of the two questions is worth 25 per cent. In Section B each question is worth 7 per cent, because you are required to answer seven of the 10 set.

- The second key piece of information in the rubric is that *you must answer seven questions in Section B*. Failure to do so will result in failing the examination. Failure to achieve *40 per cent over both sections* will also result in a fail.

Remember: the examiner will be requiring you to apply the BACKUP framework to your answers (see Chapter 1).

- **B**usiness orientation: contextualise your answer in the business context supplied or one with which you are familiar, focusing on results.

- **A**pplication **C**apability: be decisive and confident of your recommendations and solutions.

- **K**nowledge of subject matter: demonstrate that you totally understand the tools or techniques or concepts you are using.

- **U**nderstanding: recognise the implications or limitations of the concepts and tools both now and in the (scenario's) future.

- **P**ersuasion and presentation skills: present systematic and cogent arguments and discussions.

Select the questions you are going to tackle

Take a deep breath and scan your paper again. From the notes you have made on the second reading you ought to be in a position to identify the questions you mean to tackle. You will be surprised at the number of ideas that flood into your mind. It is always best to tackle the question you know most about first. This will build your confidence, but be careful not to spend so much time on this question that the rest suffer.

Allocate time

Because the whole paper takes two hours to complete, you have 24 minutes for each question in Section A and nine minutes per question in Section B. This allows nine minutes for planning and rounding off. It is essential that these timings are strictly adhered to. A common fault in the examination is the failure of students to manage their timing. Use your watch to time your answers, or at the top of the page write the scheduled completion time for that question.

It need not matter if you do not completely finish answering a question – come back to it later, using the extra time you have allocated for rounding off. But at the appropriate, scheduled time, move on religiously to the next question. You must be ruthless with yourself – time is short, and there is much to do in the exam.

Use the 30-second planner to plan your answers

Many of the questions will fall into a familiar format. Get used to answering with a short introduction covering one or two points. Then write the middle section, covering three or four points that are then developed. Follow this with a conclusion or recommendation of one or two points. This format (presented diagrammatically in Figure 5) can be adapted to almost any question and gives you a sequence for answering. You will also find that additional points occur to you for inclusion once you start writing. These can be fitted in to your plan.

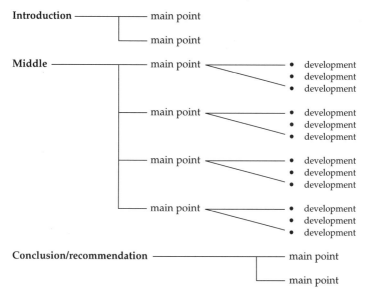

Using this approach to planning your answer you ought to be able to insert the main points within 30 seconds. Many points can be added to the outline and developed to give you answer structure and coherence.

Figure 5 Template for answering exam questions

The contents of the plan will be determined by what the question asks for.

Answering the question

This approach gives you every chance to answer the question asked by the examiner. In Section B you will be required to have a broad understanding of concepts and techniques, and these will form the basis of many of your answers. But in addition to showing an understanding of a concept or technique, it is also necessary to apply it to the scenario given. Many students fail to do this, and therefore lose valuable marks.

Look for easy marks

A computation question can help gain early marks in that you will be credited for the working that you do. Make sure it is clear in both size and completeness. This helps the examiner give you marks. The examiner is interested in the breadth of your knowledge. You will not be able to produce the perfect answer in the time allocated, so do not try.

Some parts of the question may cause you difficulties. Do not panic. Do not waste time on them – leave them until later. You can always come back to them. This is a reasonable ploy because you will still be confident. You might even experience the 'penny-dropping' syndrome by which your brain kicks in once it has relaxed and does not feel under so much pressure. (See Figure 6 on the following page.)

Present a tidy paper

Use headings and subheadings in essay-type questions. Underlining the headings gives them some importance. Avoid scoring out. If you have to delete something, however, bracket the word or phrase and draw one line through it. Leave a blank line between paragraphs. This makes it easier for the examiner to read and mark, and creates an impression of space and structure. Start each question on a fresh page, with the question number clearly identifiable in the margin. Sometimes examiners are not quite sure which question is being attempted, which as you might imagine causes problems. You will not be given the benefit of any doubt.

Section B

1. You are keen to introduce statistical control charts to monitor absence, sickness and labour turnover in your department. Your colleagues are not keen to do this. Identify the key points you would make in trying to persuade them. Justify your response.

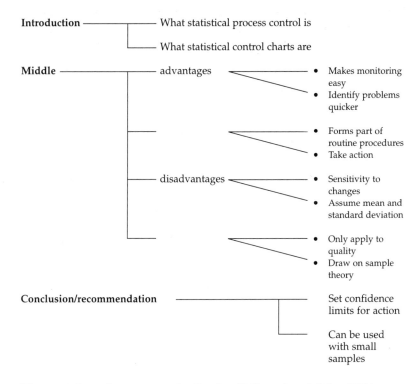

Figure 6 Sample structure for Section B Question 1, May 2004

Stay in the exam for the full time

Two hours is not long, and you can use any spare time you have left reviewing or rounding off your answers. Check your paper. Make sure it has all the correct details filled in on the front. Make sure each question you have attempted is clearly marked so that examiners know which question they are marking. You might even spend the time underlining headings or putting titles onto diagrams. These finishing touches are important because they help create the right impression.

Do not hold exam post-mortems

These serve only to dent your confidence. Remember: there is no single right answer. There are good answers and weak answers. What you have written down is relevant to you and your interpretation of a question based on your studying and experiences. These will necessarily be different from someone else's, and who is to say that his or her answer is any worthier than yours? Feel confident. You have done the best you can. It is now up to the examiners to judge your performance. Most candidates know within themselves how well they have performed in an examination. The more examinations you sit, the more accurate that feeling becomes.

Do not feel bad

At the end of the day, other people will have found the exam equally as difficult or as easy. Relax and enjoy yourself. Forget about the exam until the results are issued. Life goes on!

The preceding sections of this chapter have been prepared to provide you with help with your revision and sitting of the examination. They are based on the experience of coaching very many students through professional examinations over a number of years. The suggestions and methods outlined do work, as a good number of successful candidates will attest. They will therefore work for you too.

3 EXAMINER'S INSIGHTS

In the first part of this chapter you will find general guidance on the assessment process for this examination, reflecting the values and underlying frameworks of the Professional Development Scheme.

In the second part, more specific guidance will be provided on the examination itself, taking you through the sections of the paper, clarifying general expectations and underlining some of the reasons for poor examination performance.

Assessment

Introduction

The aim of this section is to provide insights into how you will be assessed in the Professional Development Scheme (PDS) Managing Information (MI) examination.

The underlying framework for assessment of the PDS examination is designed to assess whether you have achieved:

- the level of analytical thinking required of a postgraduate student

- the level of a CIPD professional as a 'thinking performer'

- the level of a 'business partner'

- the five BACKUP competencies.

In the following sections we endeavour to show you in general terms what you have to do to meet these criteria in the Managing Information examination.

Postgraduate criteria

The PDS MI examination paper is set and marked at post-graduate level. This means that in answering questions you must demonstrate:

- an ability to analyse issues using appropriate concepts and theoretical constructs

- a critical awareness of the role that this field of study (that is, information) plays in the management of people and organisations

- a comprehensive understanding of problem-solving methodologies and techniques appropriate to information management

- an awareness of the incompleteness and limitations of knowledge and theory in relation to organisational complexity.

You must also show that you can

- handle complex issues in a systematic and creative way, while being aware of the dynamics of a problem/issue and consequently aware also of the often-temporary nature of solutions

- plan and advise on the implementation of any proposals

- communicate your conclusions lucidly to specialist and non-specialist audiences.

At postgraduate level you must be aware that concepts and theories can be thought of as mental constructs of reality. These constructs may, however, in many circumstances not capture the complexity of reality, since they are likely to be reductionist to some degree.

This is summed up by in systems thinking by the expression:

'as if' does not/is unlikely to equal 'is'

This is the idea that concepts and theories do not deal with the whole of the complexity of a problem. This realisation should lead you on to question how good the particular theory or mental construct is, and hence what limitations can be inferred.

Concepts and theories should thus be thought of as providing insights, but not (except in the most simple of circumstances) total solutions. For example, 'rational decision-making' is not a universal recipe or description for all organisational decision-making activity as it occurs in reality. Similarly, the net present value method of project appraisal may not cover all aspects of the problem (for example, soft/people issues) and there may be some difficulty in setting discount values and accurately assessing cash flows.

In philosophical terminology, you must be *epistemologically* aware.

The 'thinking performer'

As a 'thinking performer' you should possess and display:

- a willingness to view learning as an opportunity to enhance your understanding and perception of the world around you

- an ability to apply this learning to organisational problems and to evaluate your experience

- an ability to modify and develop your thinking, if necessary, in the light of this experience

- an ability to approach problems holistically, so as to avoid a narrow reductionist focus

- an ability to adopt an eclectic approach to problem solving, leading to creative and novel solutions.

The 'business partner'

This module strongly supports the notion of the CIPD practitioner as business partner, in providing the basic understanding of business systems and analytical skills to enable practitioners to network with other stakeholders. Through networking you can learn from other stakeholders, appreciate their differing perspectives, and so collaborate with them to achieve added value for the organisation. This learning and awareness of the business partner role should be reflected in answers to questions in the MI paper.

BACKUP competencies

Many of the elements mentioned above can be encapsulated in the five key competencies highlighted in the BACKUP framework, described below.

Business orientation

For this module, business orientation involves demonstrating an understanding of the contribution/added value effective information management makes to the business or service organisation.

Evidence of reflective practice is also part of the business orientation competence:

- a capacity to learn by reflecting on one's experience

- the ability to appreciate and take account of stakeholder perspectives

- a constructively critical approach to ideas generally.

Application capability

This means demonstrating understanding of the way in which concepts, theories, frameworks or approaches can be used to tackle problems and provide insights on which to base practical actions or recommendations.

Knowledge of the subject matter

Such knowledge can be demonstrated by providing explicit evidence of how the module concepts are being used to undertake the analysis. To use a metaphor: there should be 'footprints' of the MI knowledge indicators visible throughout your answer script.

Understanding

A level of understanding of the subject matter should be attained in which the effectiveness, comprehensiveness and value of a theory technique or methodology is appreciated. This corresponds to an understanding of what kind of problem the technique/concept is a response to, and what it can and cannot do to help in problem-solving: that is, how good a fit it is and what its limitations are. In problems that exhibit 'soft' complexity, an ability to understand different perspectives should also be demonstrated.

Preparation and packaging skills

To demonstrate this competence you must be able to organise your material in a coherent way overall, appropriate for the intended audience. This means presenting a clear layout and organisation of sections, with appropriate use of diagrams and tables. Overall coherence presupposes the existence of a reasoned argument, a clear style of writing, and the adducing of valid evidence.

Examination guidance

Introduction

This section contains the examiners' comments on how to achieve the performance level needed to pass the examination. These comments are based on the experience of marking candidates' papers and preparing examiner's reports for review by the CIPD.

The examination is set and marked at postgraduate level, and the criteria that all postgraduates must meet have been covered in the previous section of this chapter. These criteria should be borne in mind constantly when writing examination answers.

The MI examination tests candidates primarily on the knowledge indicators. Although some operational indicators can be tested directly, other operational indicators are tested indirectly or by proxy, using the frequent question requirement for action planning and reference to organisational experience.

The examination is not intended to test computational skills, so you do not have to carry out any elaborate calculations. You may, however, need or want to make some very elementary calculations to demonstrate or explain a process – for example payback or NPV for a capital project evaluation. For this reason you should have a calculator with you in the examination.

Similarly, you are not expected to remember statistical formulae, so for the examination you should ensure that the examination centre provides you with the standard statistical formula sheet approved by the CIPD. You may need these formulae to remind you of aspects of a technique, if you are asked to provide an explanation. You should also be provided with tables, which likewise may help you to explain or illustrate, say, critical chi-squared values, or remind you of the hypothesis-testing process.

To summarise: the examination is intended to test your under-standing of concepts and models, their application, the interpretation of the outputs or results so obtained and their limitations: that is, the extent to which the concepts or models are able to match the variety/complexity of the perceived problem situation.

The examination paper

The MI examination is in two parts, succinctly described as Section A and Section B. Two questions must be answered in Section A. The first is a compulsory question that centres on a case study – a scenario in which many business and organisational details are given, and which presents a problem or a situation that requires resolution. The examinee is asked to provide that resolution, using the information given and the knowledge and techniques that have been studied, with recommendations, projected costs and commentary on alternative possibilities.

The candidate is given a choice between two other questions. One question will be based on a statistical problem and the other on a financial or accounting situation.

Section B of the paper comprises 10 questions, of which the candidate must answer seven as fully and as competently as possible, again demonstrating the knowledge and techniques that have been studied. Examinees might benefit from the reflection that these questions also each represent a mini-scenario, and that they are effectively asked to fulfil a role in that scenario in a realistic – and therefore professional – manner.

In both Section A and Section B of the MI paper, questions are set on the performance indicators and primarily on the knowledge indicators. Since performance indicators do not represent discrete tasks but areas of competence and understanding that are closely interrelated in real life, a single question often tests more than one indicator.

It should also be understood that a Standard's indicative content does not represent a CIPD-recommended syllabus. It simply offers an extended explanation of the relevant performance indicators.

Section A

Rationale

In Section A of this paper, you will be required to answer two questions, one of which is based on a short, unseen case study. The case study is intended to assess:

• knowledge of the module concepts, theories and methodologies

- appropriate application of these concepts, theories and methodologies explicitly to support the analysis of the case study

- the ability, from the analysis and the application of module ideas generally, to draw insights into possible solutions and their dysfunctions or emergent and possibly unforeseen consequences

- the ability to present solutions and proposals for action in a coherent and practical way.

The second question you answer in Section A will encompass either the financial/accounting or statistical component of the knowledge indicators, depending on of the two alternatives you choose. Here you will be required to write a commentary or report which interprets and explains the underlying concepts of a set of financial/accounting or statistical information in a given scenario. This question is designed to assess:

- the recognition of relevant techniques/concepts being applied in the scenario

- the ability to explain the purpose of the techniques/concepts

- the ability to interpret the results obtained in using the techniques/concepts and to point out the limitations of the information so obtained

- the ability to see the issue in a wide context and from different perspectives

- the ability to present information to an appropriate audience in a clear and concise way

- the ability to make recommendations where required.

In order to demonstrate the achievement of these objectives for the case study you should:

- read the case study carefully and identify relevant issues and primary organisational tasks

- identify the broad organisational context of the problem

- follow the case study question requirements carefully

- set your answer in the form asked for (that is, as a report, a commentary, a presentation to management, and so forth)

- ensure that you make explicit use of theoretical constructs in your analysis.

In answering the question covering the financial or statistical component of the module you should, in order to demonstrate the achievement of the assessment objectives:

- read the scenario carefully and with the question requirements in mind

- explicitly identify the financial/accounting principles or statistical techniques being used

- clearly explain the technique as required in the wording of the question

- evaluate the results of the application in a clear way, pointing out any limitations to the principles or technique and their influence within the overall business context.

Examiners' guidance to answering the case study question

The first question in Section A is based on a short, unseen case study and involves writing a report on the information issues described in the case scenario.

Candidates should structure their reports in both a systematic (logical) and systemic (using systems thinking) way. The first step should be to analyse the case study by carefully reading through it and pulling out the key issues relating to the task set in the question. This analysis stage might well conclude with a problem definition statement or, taking the development a step further, a system description. It might be useful to support this first stage with a systems map, in which the problem variables are identified.

The next step is to consider options that constitute a response to the problem stated or identified. Usually this involves suggesting types of system that would provide the information or reports to support decision-making in the management areas described in the case. Candidates might use, for example, the hierarchical model, which identifies systems on the basis of organisational levels:

- transactional systems (operational level)

- management information systems (tactical level)

- executive information systems (strategic level)

- decision-support systems (project management).

Alternatively, a database management system might be proposed, with suggestions as to the standard reports that might be produced to support decision-making.

Following this, the report might go on to consider implementation issues.

You might recognise this three-step approach as a simple version of the classic problem-solving method. Other specific information systems design methods could, however, be used, notably the Structured Systems Analysis and Design Method (SSADM), the Structured Analysis and Design of Information Systems (STRADIS), the Soft Systems Method (SSM) or Effective Technical and Human Implementation of Computer-based Systems (ETHICS). These methods are described succinctly in Chapter 6 of Elliot's *Global business information technology*, one of the recently published suggested readings.

The first two of the methods mentioned (SSADM and STRADIS) are at the 'hard' end of the information systems methods; the second two methods (SSM and ETHICS) are at the 'soft' end. Bear in mind, however, that the SSM is a problem-solving method that falls into the category of 'problem-solving as a debate'. It is more process than solution-oriented, since its primary output is an agenda for action to be discussed with the problem owner, who for cultural or historical reasons may not necessarily agree with suggested actions. It is also intended for use in very complex situations variously described as 'soft' (Checkland) or 'wicked' (Ritter, Mason and Mitroff) – that is, where the problem or the main issue has yet to be clearly defined and where stakeholders have a number of different perspectives on the problem scenario.

In the case studies for this examination the problem is usually clearly defined, so SSM is unlikely to be an appropriate approach to be used in its entirety without considering time implications. However, parts of the method might be used – for example, the 'rich picture' as a situation summary, the root definition as a specification for the system, and the conceptual model as a template. This kind of approach is categorised in the literature as SSM2: a more flexible, less mechanistic use of the original seven-stage method.

Any systems that you propose should be outlined using diagrams – for example, systems maps, context diagrams, document or data-flow diagrams, block-flow diagrams –and appropriate supporting commentary. An indication of the content of at least some of the outputs generated by the information systems should also be given.

Given the time available for this question, it is unlikely that you will be able to produce much more than a top-level data-flow diagram (DFD), in which the processes are major system functions, to be described in more detail by lower level DFDs. Context and document-flow diagrams might represent a good alternative. The application of some of these diagrams is well illustrated in Chapter 5 of Elliott (2004).

In answering the case study – and other questions in the paper – you should provide explicit evidence of careful and thoughtful study of the relevant part of the syllabus. At Master's level, credit cannot be given for thinking of a course concept – it has to be used explicitly to structure the analysis and any recommendations. You must also appreciate that an examination is a somewhat artificial setting in which you have to display your knowledge and competence, rather than just use it discreetly as you might, for example, in a work report.

Performance standards

Performance standards being tested in the case study question are:

- to be able to construct data models for analysis and design of simple information systems (a)

- to understand and explain systems concepts (d), elementary database concepts (e), the range and nature of organisational information systems (f).

Examination performance in the case study question

The main reasons for poor performance are:

- an unfocused, disorderly response to the question and poor use of report format

- no evidence of understanding and explicit application of infor- mation systems and general systems theory concepts, leading to a descriptive and anecdotal, rather than analytical, approach

- an unsystematic approach to the case study and no evidence of the use of a problem-solving method

- insufficiently detailed proposed systems

- diagrams that are poorly presented and unconventional and even sketchy, providing no insights into the problem or the proposed solution.

Examiners' guidance to answering the second question in Section A

Here you may decide to answer either the financial/accounting or the statistical question. Whichever you choose, the intention of the examiners is to assess whether you are able to recognise the finan- cial/accounting or statistical model being used, explain what it does, and interpret the information that it produces.

A typical scenario is a report that 'your manager has received'. He or she requires you to explain certain parts of the report which have been highlighted and 'which he or she does not understand'.

For the statistical question, you must demonstrate that you understand what the technique can and cannot do. In other words, if the problem to which it is being applied is too complex for the capabilities of the technique (that is, has more variables than the technique can cope with) you should make it obvious that you have recognised this. What this means is that you must be aware of the limitations of each technique, and must be prepared to point them out in your answer. It might also be the case that there are certain hidden or implicit assumptions in the technique that should be indi- cated and explained. Such a demonstration of understanding and critical awareness is a typical requirement of the postgraduate level of answers to questions.

The same things apply if you answer the financial/accounting question. For example, you may be asked to look at a report on a capital project evaluation that has used the net present value approach. Here you would need to explain the model and to discuss its strengths and weaknesses. Above all, you would be expected to identify the parts of the problem scenario that 'it did not reach' and to compare it with other models, for instance cost–benefit analysis, which have a different set of advantages and disadvantages and could deal better with other variables in the problem scenario.

Performance standards

Performance standards being tested in the Section A statistics question are:

- to be able to interpret statistical information for management (d)
- to understand and explain basic statistical concepts (j).

And for the Section A finance/accounting question:

- to understand and explain financial statements (h)
- to be able to interpret basic trading accounts (f)
- to decide on financial performance standards (g).

Section B

Rationale

Section B of the paper is designed to assess the whole range of standards for this module. The format of the questions often represents realistic 'critical incident' scenarios to which you are required to respond succinctly but convincingly. Typically, questions use e-mail, telephone message, memo, meetings and 'your own organisation' (or one with which you are familiar either directly or through reading or networking) as the basis for a question.

These 'situational' formats mean that the questions give a strong feeling of being in a real-life situation, and require the candidate to respond professionally to the demands of that situation. It is important to understand that you must not focus on the process of answering but on the content implicit in the scenario, bearing in mind the objectives of the assessment as outlined at the beginning of this chapter.

In this part of the examination paper there is an expectation that in the area of information technology, decision-making processes, problem-solving and system design methodologies, you will be up to date with current developments and applications in the personnel and development area, both in your own organisation and generally, through regular reading of *People Management*, the business press and other management journals. With the statistical component, an advanced knowledge of techniques – for example, multivariate correlation – is not required, but knowledge of current applications of statistical analysis/modelling in your organisation is considered important and will be expected. Likewise for the financial component, knowledge of current applications of finance/accounting principles in the field of human resource management and in your organisation will be required.

Examiners' guidance to answering Section B questions

In this section of the paper you are required to answer seven out of the 10 questions listed. These questions are designed to test the whole range of standards for this module and are equally divided between the four main sections of the indicative knowledge content.

It is essential that you make a valid attempt at seven questions. In order to do this you must be familiar with most of the topics in the indicative content. It is important to remember that if one of your seven answers is not relevant to the question asked, it may be viewed as an altogether invalid answer, and you may receive a fail grade.

As outlined above, the format of the questions often represents critical incident scenarios (for instance, e-mail, telephone, memo, meetings) to which you are required to respond succinctly and convincingly.

In order to provide suitably detailed answers within the examination time limits, you may use diagrams, flowcharts and bullet point formats. Although diagrams are a useful aid to overcoming time limitations, you should not view them as a complete answer in themselves. In most cases, some brief commentary, accompanying explanation or (more likely) discussion is needed. Similarly, you should be aware that the overuse of bullet points often results in a fragmented answer, and the coherence of the argument or the relationship between the bullet points may then not be apparent to the examiner. Bullet point answers do need some accompanying 'continuity scripting'.

As with questions in Section A, you must display explicit knowledge of the relevant models, concepts, techniques and frameworks in your answers and remember to adopt a critical, 'thinking performer' approach whenever the opportunity arises. This means that in most of your answers there should be a discursive element. You should also illustrate points in your answer with reference to your organisation and to either theoretical and/or practice literature.

Exam success in Section B

In order to achieve success in Section B the following features should normally be discernible in your answers:

- explicit use of relevant literature (theories, concepts, models, frameworks) as a basis for any analysis

- reflection on choice of concepts, theories and models – and critical evaluation in terms of, for example, their internal logic, the evidence to support them and their applicability

- the use of relevant examples to show how concepts might be applied and reflection on this application and any consequential implementation problems

- the use of material that draws on wider reading, for example critical debates on the validity or scope of theories or concepts, alternative theories or concepts, interesting or novel applications, and different perspectives of the problem or issue.

The grading structure: grade profiles

In marking PDS examination answers and scripts overall, examiners will be using the following grade profiles:

Distinction

- Comprehensive coverage of each aspect of the question – a completely focused answer.

- Compelling evidence that the candidate thoroughly understands all the issues and can explain their full significance by reference to good practice.

- In general, meets the highest professional standards in this area of the Standards.

Merit

- Essential points have been covered and related as necessary to context.

- Clear evidence that the candidate understands what the concepts/techniques referred to in the question mean, and their significance in broad terms.

- A good explanation is given of each of the points made.

- Overall, an answer that is not at distinction level, but that nonetheless is well balanced, impresses as being well informed and convincingly relates theory to practice where required.

Pass

- Essential points have been covered.

- Convinces as being useful and along the right lines even if some of the detail is sketchy.

- Overall, an answer that deals with the main aspects of the question competently if not with any particular originality or flair.

Marginal fail

- Insufficient numbers of the essential points have been covered.

- Candidate is able to describe situations adequately but is not able to relate them to the specific context set in the question.

- An answer along the right lines but too generalised/thin for a pass.

Outright fail

- An answer that is so flawed that it cannot be regarded as having even marginal potential.

- Candidate does not demonstrate the level of competence expected in a qualified HR professional.

Common reasons for low exam grades and failure

Candidates who fail to achieve their full potential in the MI examination display some of the following weaknesses:

- Failure to respond directly to the questions and wasting precious examination time putting in irrelevant material. This is often an attempt to 'write themselves' into the answer, hoping they will stumble on something relevant, instead of carefully thinking out what is being asked for and making an outline plan.

- (Closely related to the first point is) over-elaboration of some answers at the expense of others. The law of diminishing returns operates here: excessive detail in one answer is unlikely to attract as many marks as providing full answers to all questions. This applies particularly in Section B.

- Failure to explain concepts clearly and demonstrate an understanding of the scope and limitations in their application.

- Failure to base answers explicitly on concepts and theories.

- Failure to illustrate the answer with organisational examples when requested to do so.

- Failure to provide sufficiently discursive answers – a tendency to naivety and simple description in tackling complex questions.

- Ignoring, or failing to make explicit reference to, the context or question scenario and simply citing theoretical material.

- Failure to understand that freedom to interpret the question in one's own way is not freedom to answer a different question.

- Failure to recognise what knowledge is being requested in the question, due to unfamiliarity with the module material.

- Attempts to provide answers that could have been written purely on the basis of common sense and show no knowledge or application of module material.

Finally, it must be said that those who mark the examination papers generally have a very supportive approach, trying to find ways to give you marks for what you know. So all you have to do is to provide evidence that you have acquired a good range of ideas, skills and insights about information management and statistics. But you do have to do it.

SECTION 3

EXAMINATION PRACTICE
AND FEEDBACK

4 EXAMINATION QUESTIONS AND FEEDBACK

Introduction

This chapter is designed to help you tackle the Managing Information (MI) examination questions. It should be noted that the feedback given on each question does not constitute a model answer, but highlights some of the issues that ought to have been addressed. Wherever possible, computations will be carried out to help those of you who feel that this is an area of particular weakness. Remember: there are weak answers, good answers and better answers. This section concentrates on helping you to develop your thinking and consequently to improve the way you tackle questions in the future. Some of the more common pitfalls will be pointed out.

Section A questions are based on a mini-case study and some computation. The examiner requires your answer in a report format. This is important to remember, because failing to provide the correct format will lose you one or two marks. You should also be spending around 25 minutes tackling each question you choose. The choice is narrow, for Question 1 is compulsory, leaving you to also choose either Question 2 or Question 3.

Section B questions are designed to cover a broader spectrum of the course. Candidates are expected to answer seven shorter questions from the 10 that are set. In general terms you will be spending something like seven or eight minutes per question. This is essential in this area, for students frequently fail to read the rubric at the beginning of the paper and tackle fewer than seven questions. This of course means that they fail the paper. Be warned, then – time management of this particular examination is crucial to your success. Practising answering seven questions within one hour is good preparation for this part of the exam.

First we look at all the questions in the November 2003 exam, then at the finance-oriented questions from both the November 2003 and May 2004 exams.

November 2003 MI exam: Section A

Question I

John Naughton has recently been recruited as general manager of Aircraft Services plc, a family business that provides maintenance services for medium sized corporate aircraft and he has retained you as Information Technology (IT) consultant.

The company was founded some 20 years ago at a single site location, but since then has expanded to four sites located at major airports across the UK. It employs 60 highly qualified airframe and engine technicians. Each site is managed by an engineering manager.

The company has deservedly attained a reputation for offering an impeccable, highly personalised customer service. Company representatives meet charter customers at the airport, quickly complete a service order and then arrange accommodation for the pilot during servicing of the aircraft. The company attempts to minimise the time the aircraft is out of service and prides itself on solving mechanical problems quickly and with a high level of reliability.

John has completed a review of the management of all the centres and has been pleasantly surprised with the general level of performance. Although the business seems to be running smoothly at present, he knows that future success depends on increasing its efficiency, while continuing to ensure personalised service.

In addition, the board wishes to expand the business and John knows that the manual system for recording customer requests, repair schedules, regular aircraft maintenance and customer billing is antiquated and will hinder these expansion plans.

John has noted in his reflective diary that technological developments in the field of avionics are going to require on going technical education and training of the current workforce. Furthermore, future workforce planning will involve the recruitment of professional aeronautical and electronic engineers.

He is also aware that testing the latest equipment is becoming elaborate. Upgrading the workshops with the latest in ultrasonics and lasers is something that cannot be put off for long. Convincing the board of the need to take decisions on this and other important expansion projects may need some sophisticated decision support.

John has briefed you on his review of the company and his ideas. He tells you that his prime concern is to have the systems that enable his managers to plan and control the operations effectively from a technical and cost viewpoint. He also wants an overview of what is going on at each maintenance centre and information to plan for future developments.

He has asked you as a consultant to write a report on the information needs of the organisation in the future.

The knowledge indicators for this question are:

• Systems concepts SYST 1 and SYST 2.

The learning outcomes are:

• to be able to construct data models for analysis and design simple information systems

• to understand and explain system concepts

• to understand and explain elementary database concepts

• to understand and explain the range and nature of organisational information systems.

In tackling a question of this nature perhaps you could identify the key words. These we have done as an example, by using a highlighter as we read the blurb. The list is given in Table 2.

Table 2 Key words for November 2003 Section 1 Question 1

Key words in text	Reason for choice
four sites located at major airports	(need for co-ordination of information, perhaps standardisation)
success depends on increasing its efficiency	(need for control, simplicity and ease of operation);
wish to expand the business	(therefore more information in future, strategic level?);

Table 2 continued

manual system	(something already in place to work with);
recording customer requests and customer billing	(record keeping and control, organisational level?);
repair schedules and regular maintenance	(operational level, project management?);
future workforce planning	(manpower planning, strategic level, operational level);
testing equipment	(operational level);
plan and control the operation effectively. know what is going on	(operational and tactical levels strategic level);
sophisticated decision support	(MIS, Project management, database management systems, Dataflow Modelling, Relational data analysis systems)

By approaching the question in this manner, you can quickly begin to clarify the structure of your answer. From my table, which took less than two minutes to construct, it is evident that the information needs of Aircraft Services plc are at three different levels:

- *Strategic*: looking towards expansion, developing policy for the four sites, and know what is going on.

- *Tactical*: looking at management information to enable the organisation to operate efficiently and cost effectively.

- *Operational*: looking at the day-to-day systems that enable interaction between different facets of the business; customers, determining work loads; equipment testing and other business controls.

This should focus your answer towards a simple information system of a hierarchical structure. You could however use your knowledge of SSADM as the basis of your system and show how you would apply this concept to the question. The major pitfall in this essay is that you begin to describe everything you know about designing systems.

Remember the question asks for a report on the information needs of the future, therefore you will need to include some balanced argument identifying the pros and cons for a small family concern such as Aircraft Services plc. Uppermost in your mind ought to be cost, effectiveness, efficiency, timings, acceptance testing, system handover and so on. The models identified in the core text (Bee and Bee 1999, ch6) provide a good theoretical foundation to underpin your knowledge. In addition a good diagram outlining your approach helps to provide you with a solid logical framework (see Figure 7).

It never ceases to amaze me how many candidates do not understand the instruction 'write a report'. Once again the chief examiner

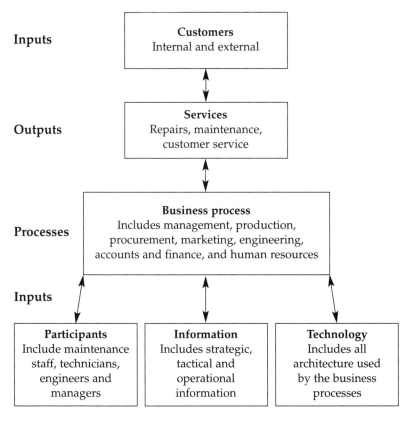

Figure 7 Diagram for Section A Question 1, November 2003

highlights this as a characteristic of weak answers. It should not be a problem, because all students should be programmed to write or follow conventional report formats. Marks need not be lost easily. It is therefore paramount that you check that you know a simple report format and use it in your answer. Make this a prerequisite of your study for the examination.

A basic diagram could follow a work-centred analysis approach (WCA) similar to Stephen Alter's model in *Information systems: a management perspective* (1997). This begins from the perspective of the organisation as a system.

This approach helps you maintain a balanced view, focusing on the requirements of each element of the organisation while homing in on the issues that are most relevant to Aircraft Services plc. It also shows the interrelationship of each aspect of the model.

John must focus at a strategic level and also develop some project management capability, to provide direction for the business. The engineering managers need to concentrate on the operational and tactical levels to provide management information that will enable the business to run smoothly and effectively. Operationally, this will include repair and maintenance information, purchase and usage of material information, customer information, costs and profitability, quality and service targets, staffing and training requirements and equipment reliability, timescales for individual projects at each centre location, routines for daily efficiency of the repair and maintenance operation, and dealing with clients.

At the tactical level, information is likely to be about determining which aspects of the business to develop, what additional equipment will be required to extend the service provision, how each centre is utilised to maximise its capacity and capability, and personnel decisions related to training and development, recruitment and remuneration of highly skilled engineers and professional aeronautical personnel.

In contrast, John will require information at a strategic level that will help him make long-term decisions for the overall company, and select and formulate organisational objectives for each site location. In order to keep up to date with technological change in the aerospace industry, provision for environment scanning may be incorporated into the system.

When using a diagram or system you will need to remember the following.

- Show the integrative nature of the system. This means that it should clearly indicate how each level fits into the next.

- Your system should cover each of the hierarchical levels.

- You should contextualise the diagram to make it relevant to the scenario you have been given – you should not generalise.

Although the system shown in Figure 8 indicates the nature of information required at each level of the decision-making process, some

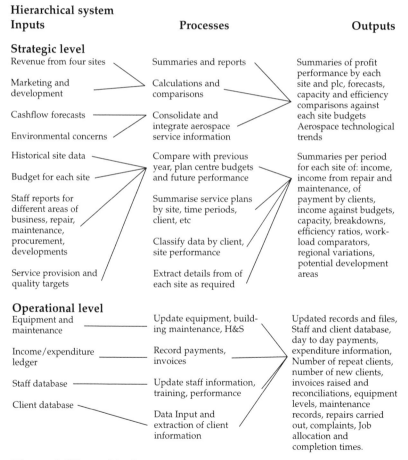

Hierarchical system

Inputs	Processes	Outputs
Strategic level		
Revenue from four sites	Summaries and reports	Summaries of profit performance by each site and plc, forecasts, capacity and efficiency comparisons against each site budgets Aerospace technological trends
Marketing and development	Calculations and comparisons	
Cashflow forecasts	Consolidate and integrate aerospace service information	
Environmental concerns		
Historical site data	Compare with previous year, plan centre budgets and future performance	Summaries per period for each site of: income, income from repair and maintenance, of payment by clients, income against budgets, capacity, breakdowns, efficiency ratios, workload comparators, regional variations, potential development areas
Budget for each site		
Staff reports for different areas of business, repair, maintenance, procurement, developments	Summarise service plans by site, time periods, client, etc	
	Classify data by client, site performance	
Service provision and quality targets	Extract details from of each site as required	
Operational level		
Equipment and maintenance	Update equipment, building maintenance, H&S	Updated records and files, Staff and client database, day to day payments, expenditure information, Number of repeat clients, number of new clients, invoices raised and reconciliations, equipment levels, maintenance records, repairs carried out, complaints, Job allocation and completion times.
Income/expenditure ledger	Record payments, invoices	
Staff database	Update staff information, training, performance	
Client database	Data Input and extraction of client information	

Figure 8 Hierarchical system

consideration must be given to how that information is controlled. It would be astute to use the control model as a framework for your answer. This would identify the key areas of the system where controls need to operate.

Question 2

The Human resources (HR) team in your medium organisation would like to invest in a Human Resources Information System (HRIS). Your management services department has written a report on this project, which includes the following executive summary, together with the diagram and information below it.

Executive Summary: Currently information costs per employee are £150. With the current numbers, the cost per employee for the new HRIS would be £200. There is, however, an 80 per cent chance of a major expansion in the near future and without the new HRIS, this would mean that the current information costs would be sub-contracted. Information costs per employee in the expanded organisation would reduce to £100, however if the new HRIS were to be installed.

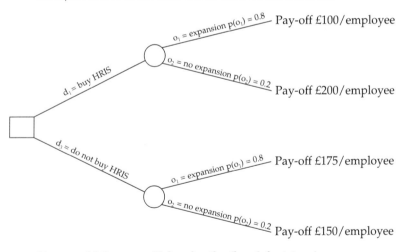

Expected Monetary Value for the 'buy' decision is:
    (0.8 x 100) + (0.2 x 200) = £120
Expected Monetary Value for the 'do not buy' decision is:
    (0.8 x 175) + (0.2 x 150) = £170

Write a report for your HR team explaining what all this means. Discuss whether or not you should take this information into account in making your decision.

This question at first sight is quite off-putting, but on closer inspection it is actually straightforward, focusing on using a decision analysis approach.

The question basically wants the exam candidate:

- to be able to interpret statistical information for management

- to be able to understand and explain basic statistical concepts.

The knowledge indicator is STATS 2, using statistical concepts.

The key to this question is to write an explanatory report for your colleagues. This means that a number of elements must be in your explanation. Doing a short brainstorm you might come up with decision theory, decision trees, expected monetary value, and risk and limitations.

Decision theory is a straightforward way of making decisions by applying a probability or payoff approach to determine the optimal (best) decision. Clearly within the answer you want to determine whether or not to invest in the HRIS. The decision will also be based on how you view the future, therefore the accompanying information is crucial, as it tells you the risk or chance factor of the event happening. The chance of a major expansion of the business and the resultant increase in staffing information is 80 per cent and this provides a low-risk option.

The 'decision tree' is constructed using this information. It starts with a decision node. We have two choices (decision branches), 'buy' the system or 'not buy' the system, which emanate from the decision node. These stop at outcome nodes. Each outcome node of the decision is constructed by using maximum and minimum decision criteria providing optimistic and pessimistic views. Hence the choice 'to buy or not' is determined by the 'no expansion' option and the 'expansion' option. This then gives us four probability options (outcome branches): buy and expand; buy and do not expand; do not buy and expand; do not buy and do not expand (remain the same). Each of these options has a monetary payoff. It is the payoff information that helps determine the final decision.

Expected monetary value uses the probabilities to provide a weighted payoff for each of the options making the decision critical dependent on the probability.

From the two monetary values provided in the exam, it is suggested that the option to buy is in fact the better option as the expected monetary value is lower.

Risk and utility however have not been taken into consideration with this decision, and the company may have to consider such issues as managerial preference, availability of finance, changes in the environment, the financial return of taking this decision (which is not calculated), compatibility with existing software, timescale for implementation, training, and switching systems.

In reality, decisions within organisations like the one described in the exam paper are rarely that simple and often are linked to other aspects of the business. It is not guaranteed that the expected monetary value will give you the 'best' solution. This is dependent on the process being repeated on numerous occasions to build a higher confidence level in the decision. With one-off approaches the probability of the uncertain variable – in this case, the likelihood of expansion – needs to be estimated more accurately. This in itself proves difficult, as there are many uncontrollable variables that may affect the estimate (see 'risk and utility' above).

November 2003 MI exam: Section B

Because time is short for these questions, you should take every opportunity to use diagrams, flowcharts (pictures often convey a thousand words) and bullet points to provide a more rounded answer. These should be supplemented by adequate commentary. The examiner goes to great lengths to point this out. Each question in itself represents a mini-scenario, and it would serve you well to remember this. You are playing a role, so respond in the way you would if you really were in that scenario. That way you will generate examples to help with your explanation of the concepts or techniques of these questions.

Question 1

What insights can information systems design methodologies provide for managers in your organisation?

You need to focus your answer to describe 'insights' for your organisation. It is no good trying to bamboozle the examiner with purely systems design jargon.

A good approach would be to talk about SSADM or one of the other methodologies like dataflow diagrams or Checklands' Soft System Methodology.

By identifying the key modules of the SSADM approach you can then go on to discuss the insights the method provides for your organisation (see Figure 9).

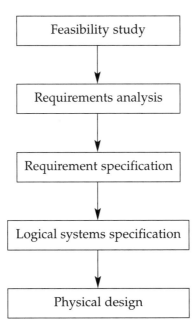

Figure 9 Key modules of the SSADM approach
Source: Weaver, Lambrou and Walkley (2002) p8.

Feasibility study

- An analysis of current problems and operation. This area is crucial. It will provide details of how the current system is not meeting the new demands of the business. It will also highlight good aspects that need not be altered because they are working well. It should also provide the designers with an understanding of the company environment, therefore matching the right technical architecture to the company's circumstances.

- At this stage a feasibility study could be produced. This will provide a high-level overview of the organisation's processing and data, looking at several options for taking the project forward, and balancing benefits against cost for each one. This gives the organisation insights into potential benefits, potential opportunities and potential developments.

Requirements analysis

- Requirements of the specification: this means distinguishing between the logical and the physical structure in order that a number of options are generated that take account of the organisation's situation. Following this, the management will be able to determine which solution will best suit its needs.

- By looking at the current system the organisation can gain insight into which elements of the system are working well and can be transferred to the new system. The support relationship that is in the current system, and the dependencies that exist, give management an insight into the sensitivity and weaknesses or strengths of the current system.

- Management within the organisation might also gain insight into the scope and complexity of the new system, and standardisation would provide a common understanding of concepts and terminology.

Requirement specification

- This provides insights into the planning process, identifying through the use of dataflow modelling, for example, organisational procedures, documentation that needs to be in place, and the clarification of roles and levels of authority.

- The understanding of events and their effects provides crucial insight into the key factors that will impinge on the business and need to be updated constantly. The continuous updating of prices within a supermarket environment is a good example here. Creating 'life histories' helps with this process and enables managers to predict and plan more effectively.

Logical systems specification

- This translates the information from the previous steps into alternative technical environments. Here it is possible to see the limitations of solutions and wake up to the reality of the enormity of the task if the solution chosen to be completely effective. Management might also gain insight into how the processes that currently operate could be streamlined.

- Database design issues must be discussed in the light of data design and process proposals. For your organisation there could be insights into areas of concern surrounding adequate database management systems that support the needs of the business.

Physical design

- At this stage the final specification should be determined, which should take into consideration the needs of the organisation, the technical environment and the user interface. Insights may be given about ergonomics, space utilisation, cost-effectiveness, capacity management and efficient handling of information. In other words, by looking at these methodologies managers within any organisation can come closer to how the operation is being run and how efficient and effective the organisation is. Strengths and weaknesses are highlighted and can inform or confirm managers' understanding of the business.

Question 2

What techniques might assist you in planning an organisation's future operations? What limitations do these techniques have?

This is a question about forecasting and not planning. The key words in the question, 'techniques', 'planning' and 'future operations', should alert you to this. Furthermore, you are required to comment on their 'limitations', so this question is in two parts. First, you need to identify some of the techniques and talk about how they can assist, then talk about their limitations.

From Chapter 15/16 in Bee (1999) you could choose from time series analysis, correlation and regression analysis, and Delphi approaches. Make sure however that you cover qualitative as well as quantitative approaches. This will give a more balanced view.

Quantitative approaches: time series analysis

Time series analysis uses historical data to see if any pattern emerges. Assumptions are then made that the pattern will continue into the future. This enables us to forecast a value at some point of time in the future. Some of the more commonly used methods are

- moving averages

- weighted moving averages

- indexed four quarter moving averages.

Each of these methods involves taking averages over 12-month periods.

The simplest method of forecasting can be to look back at the previous period sales and using *the line of 'best fit'* to extrapolate for the future. This is using linear regression effectively. Looking back at company figures is often referred to as using historical data. It would be a mistake to rely solely on historical data as the future does not mirror the past exactly, and you need to be aware of this. Nevertheless we need to use historical data intelligently to give us an indication of what future demand may be like.

Indexing is always a reliable source for forecasting, as we are able to interpolate the trends of the underlying behaviour of the figures. From this we will make judgments based on other environmental factors as to whether the pattern will remain the same in the future.

Whichever method you use for forecasting you need to be aware of anomalies in the historic information that may distort the results. Sometimes adverse weather conditions might push up the sales of umbrellas, for instance, thereby distorting the regular sales figures. If you do not know this, your forecasts are likely to be inaccurate and sometimes even wrong. Similarly, particular large 'one-off' orders have to be considered and those figures smoothed to compensate for the distortion.

Qualitative approaches: Delphi technique

This technique asks experts to best guess the future, almost like the ancients visiting Delphi to consult the 'Oracle' about their future. In the modern case the experts use a variety of other diagnostic tools to support their 'guesstimations'.

A more adventurous approach is that used in *scenario planning*, developed by Shell in the 1970s, which considered alternative ways of tackling environmental changes that could impact on its business.

Surveys of consumer intentions or sales force opinions are also used to predict future demand and the likelihood of the organisation satisfying it.

Test marketing provides information now that can be used to identify potential sales subsequent to product launch.

What is clear is that the longer the period of forecast, the greater the chance that the prediction will be wrong. It makes more sense therefore to identify a number of different detailed forecasts over shorter time spans to try to improve the accuracy of the prediction.

Limitations

When making forecasts the organisation's limiting factors must be considered. These might include:

- Limitations on the amount of finance available for expansion (for example, the company wants to build a new factory but cannot raise the capital).

- Limitations on the size of the market the company is pursuing (for example, the Isle of Man only has a population of approx 75,000 therefore opportunities are limited).

- Limitations of the machinery or equipment in terms of capacity (for example, the company may already be operating at full production capacity and unable to take any more work). A hotel is limited to the number of bedrooms it possesses and has to turn away business when it is full.

- Limitations in the skills of the workforce (for example, expansion opportunities for many companies can be in the area of information technology, yet there is a shortage of this skill worldwide). This might impinge on organisational development.

- Limitations on physical resources (for example, the projected site for the new factory might have less space than was forecast, due to planning regulations).

Question 3

Illustrate how control models can aid decision making in your organisation in either human resources or some other operational area.

A control model could be used (see Figure 10).

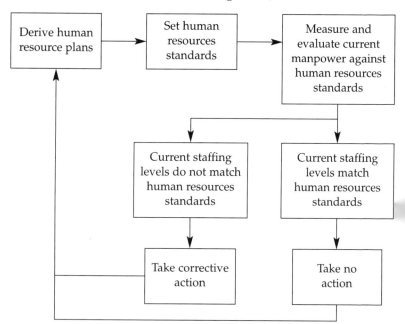

Figure 10 A control model

With a simple control diagram like this it is clear that decisions related to human resources planning could be made. By using this model the HR department can set up a number of accceptable policy standards for, say, absenteeism or sickness, and be able to monitor and control how these policies are operating within the organisation. Very quickly issues for concern can be identified, and this allows HR to make appropriate decisions for the business. In similar fashion such a system will keep track of all training and development that has been undertaken, and anomalies or skills gaps can be picked up and dealt with before they become problematic. Such control methods are essential to ensure systems and procedures are being adhered to. In HR it is necessary to keep tabs on who has done overtime and how much overtime has been completed. This information is subsequently fed into the payroll system, into HR budgets, and into the organisation's overall performance to measure effectiveness and efficiency. Therefore control with feedback potential is most desirable.

Models of control, like Lucey's double loop approach, ensure that the feedback loop is in place. These provide detection sensors that feed back throughout the system, alerting the organisation to potential dangers. The sensors usually feed back to a higher level of control so that the necessary action can be taken. In our HR example this might mean feeding back to a manager about training needs that have not yet been met. This allows the manager to make an appropriate decision based on the most up-to-date information available to him or her.

Unfortunately with all elements of control the human factor may play a part. The model is only as good as the information it provides. So if there is outdated information, for example holiday lists held on the database that are not kept up to date, the HR department will be seen not to make the appropriate decision,. This might mean that a request for particular holiday dates was denied, which would then have knock-on effects throughout the organisation.

Particularly of relevance to HR departments is the concept of feedforward control. This enables them to scan the horizon and determine how the environment might impact on the company. In particular, scanning for changes in the employment skills pool often gives HR a head start in identifying potential staff problems with recruitment and selection in the future.

Question 4

Show how information from an ogive (cumulative frequency distribution) might be used. Explain the terms, lower quartile, median and upper quartile.

This was a straightforward question, and tested knowledge and application of a particular statistical technique. Information from an ogive can give us measurements that form a summary of the behaviour of the entire population. This is achieved not merely by providing a useful display of the data but also by preparing for future operations on the data in the future.

The median

This is referred to as the middle mark when all the data is arranged in order of size. This might for example help us to determine the median age among 199 applicants for jobs. The 100th person will be of the median age. The difficulty about using this is that it might not give a true average, and could be distorted by extremely high or low-aged applicants. In the summer, for example, many students apply for work. It rarely serves a good purpose when data is difficult to measure. If we considered workers' efficiency in performing a job, the middle worker would represent median efficiency, even though we perhaps could not measure or quantify the data accurately.

The upper and lower quartiles

These help to identify how spread out the data is. As the upper and lower extremes of the data may cause distortion, we often exclude this information and look at the quartile range. This allows us to look at the scatter of the data between the upper quartile (75 per cent) and the lower quartile (25 per cent). The central quartile is of course the median. Using this approach reduces the variability of results. In addition the quartile range can convey information about the skewness of the information or the symmetric distribution. The more skewed the data is, the closer the median will be to one or other quartile. (See Figure 11.)

In the figure the lower quartile indicates that the age of the 49.5th application was between 20 and 25: probably around 23. The 100th applicant was 25, and the 149.5th application was by a person aged

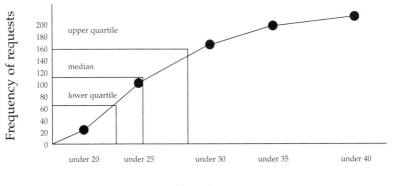

Staff applicant

Figure 11 Normative rational model approach

between 25 and 30, probably around 28. The data is skewed towards the younger age groups.

Question 5

Evaluate to what extent rational decision-making is carried out in your organisation.

Decision-making lies at the heart of management. It is an activity that is often hurried and ill-informed. At junior management level, much of the information is available to make good decisions (for example, quality-control inspections, equipment checks, credit rating of new customers, and stock checks for ordering). Many of these are done systematically and follow prescriptive methods. Few if any are made by intuition. Intuition has a place in management decision-making, in that gut feel or first impressions are often right. Such decisions can, however, be coloured by self-fulfilling prophecy or bias, where only particular qualities are investigated in, say, candidates for a job or promotion. The legal requirements dealing with recruitment issues point you in the direction of rationality and accountability. Experience can add to the decision-making process and help with interpretation, or the development of alternative approaches – but each and every one of us has different experiences, so it becomes more difficult for decisions based purely on this approach to be accepted.

The normative rational model approach gives a framework for managers to develop their decision-making abilities. Such models apply logical principles and force users down a recognised logical pathway. They work best when the organisation has a clearly defined set of objectives and goals, lending itself more to junior management decision-making rather than strategic decision-making.

Such models are often criticised for being prescriptive. The model also relies on organisations operating in a logical and rational way. There is much evidence to suggest that this is not the case. Objectives may be difficult to define, not comprehensive enough, or not sufficiently specific to help guide the decision. Decisions are often more complex and involve more than one individual. The information system within your organisation may not support the decision-making process adequately. Within many public sector organisations, objectives are well defined, and it is easy to translate these into performance criteria, therefore rational approaches are encouraged. These manifest themselves in the formal policy documents that are produced. At strategic levels within many organisations more incremental approaches are used for decision-making responding to environmental issues. It is not cost-effective to continually produce comprehensive analysis for decision-making, and organisations neither have the time nor the inclination to do so. Most are more likely to have hybrid systems that are made up of the best from all the methodologies available. (See Figure 12.)

Question 6

Assess the contribution Information Systems (IS)/Information Technology (IT) might make to innovations in your organisation.

From the model you can see that information systems provide the organisation with a transformation process that helps to handle environmental complexity. Inputs turn into outputs. For many organisations this means collecting data from outside and inside the organisation, and turning it into useful information with the help of the information user.

Information from outside the organisation is varied. At the strategic level it supports the decision-making of the organisation – identifying markets, competitor activity, social and environmental

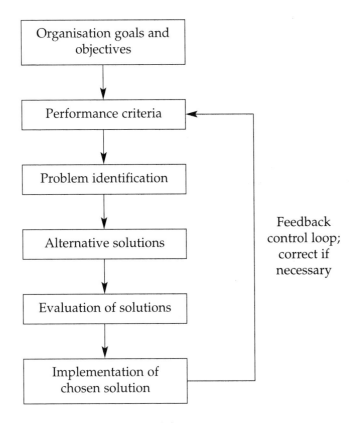

Figure 12 Information systems model

trends, new technologies – and can contribute to innovation. This information forms part of the planning process, and enables the organisation to formulate plans of action for the future; it can then filter into scenario planning or contingency planning to help determine policy and identify modes of operation.

At the tactical level, the information provided about competitor activity, new product development or new processes for manufacturing enables the organisation to be innovative and respond to and seize potential market opportunities.

At the operational level, the data gathered and processed provides timely information about service levels and customer

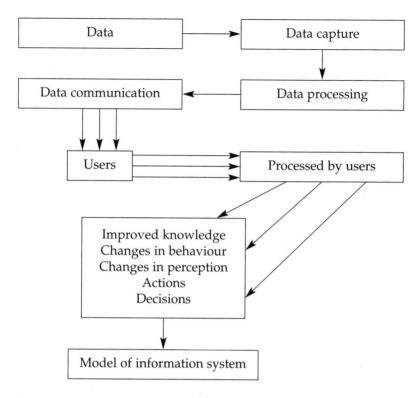

Figure 13 The IS/IT contribution

satisfaction, thereby ensuring innovative approaches can be adopted to maintain competitive advantage. This can be benchmarked with competitor information.

Internally, the data collected provides information for management reporting and decision-making. This forms part of the whole problem-solving process. Internal information contributes by providing financial information that is used to determine the effectiveness and efficiency of the organisation. Problem areas like waste management can be highlighted and tackled to improve performance and utilisation. Tactics for the continuance of the business can be developed as appropriate. At the operational level, performance information is produced to let operators know how well they are performing, and this can be the foundation for new working practices and methodologies to ameliorate the organisation's approach. Most information, however, is designed to provide feedback on the organisation's control mechanisms (for example, quality-control checks, warehouse audits, and telephone monitoring). This enables the organisation to be proactive, building a knowledge management culture where innovation is seen through commitment, capability and empowerment.

The finance questions

In looking at the questions that deal with the financial section of the MI content, we will be taking questions from both the November 2003 and May 2004 exam papers. There were four questions in each paper, one in Section A and three in Section B. Let us start by looking at the Section A questions. The November 2003 exam question covered budgeting and variance analysis, and the May 2004 question was testing your understanding of project appraisal techniques.

November 2003 MI exam: Section A finance question

Optional question 2

The following information has been prepared by your accountants for one of the manufacturing units for the year to 31 March 2003.

Fixed budget for year to 31st March 2003

Level of Activity	Budget 50%	Actual 60%
Costs	£	£
Direct materials	100,000	122,000
Direct labour	200,000	236,000
Variable overhead	20,000	28,000
Total variable cost	320,000	386,000
Fixed overhead	80,000	84,000
Total costs	400,000	470,000

Flexed budget operating statement for the year to 31st March 2003

	Fixed budget	Flexed budget	Actual costs	Variance favourable/ adverse
Activity Level	50%	60%	60%	
	£	£	£	£
Direct materials	100,000	120,000	122,000	(2,000)
Direct labour	200,000	240,000	236,000	4,000
Variable overhead	20,000	24,000	28,000	(4,000)
Total variable costs	320,000	384,000	386,000	(2,000)
Fixed overhead	80,000	80,000	84,000	(4,000)
Total costs	400,000	464,000	470,000	(6,000)

Your manager has left this information on your desk. Attached is a note asking you to explain why there is a flexed budget and what causes these sorts of variances.

Let us start by thinking about what this question is testing.

First, it is asking you to explain a 'flexed budget', and why it has been used in this company. This is an opportunity to show your knowledge, but even if you do not know what a flexed budget is you can deduce it from the data in the question!

Second, it is asking you to offer possible reasons for the variances. This means that you have to know which variances are favourable and which are adverse (the ones in brackets) and understand how a standard costing system allows you to extract the different types of variance, which are essentially price and usage variances.

Do not forget that the exam is also testing your presentation skills, so you need to make sure that your answer is clearly presented.

To answer this question you start by explaining a flexed budget and its applicability to your company. Then you need to explain what the variances are, and offer possible explanations for the variances found in the second table.

This is not designed to be a 'model answer', however a good answer should include the following aspects.

Evidence of knowledge

Of our costs, 80 per cent are variable, and consequently change with the production level. This means that when the activity level changes, these costs change. Therefore if the volumes change, the budget needs to change to reflect the expected performance at this level of activity. So when the activity rises from 50 per cent to 60 per cent you would expect the materials cost to rise from £100,000 to £120,000, as there has been a 20 per cent increase (*50 per cent to 60 per cent*) in the business's activity level. However the fixed costs remain unchanged at £80,000, as they are unaffected by the increase in activity.

The original budget was based on the budgeted activity level of 50 per cent, which has been exceeded. The flexible budget has amended the budget for the actual level of activity, enabling managers to focus on the variances that are within their control. These variances either improve the business's profitability (*favourable* variances shown as a positive number) or reduce it (*adverse* variances shown in brackets). You can see that even after amending the budget for the changed level of activity, the expenditure on materials and variable overheads increased. The labour costs were £4,000 less than expected at this activity level, and overall the business spent £2,000 more than it should have done at this activity level.

Variance analysis

You have now shown the examiner that you understand flexible budgets and why they are appropriate to this organisation. You now have to show that you know about variance analysis. Try to relate your answer to your own organisation to reinforce your business orientation. So now let us see why these variances could have occurred.

In most businesses the planned unit, or process cost, is called the 'standard cost'. This multiplies the planned costs by the planned usage at the planned level of activity to give the budgeted cost. The differences between the budgeted cost and the actual costs are called *variances*. These variances could arise from paying more than you expected (a *price* variance), or using more than you planned (a *usage* variance). However, these terms are not always used. For example, labour variances are usually described as *rate* variances (when it cost more because you have paid more) or *efficiency* variances (when something has taken longer to make than expected). The advantage of identifying these variances is that you can identify why the variances have occurred.

You can now show the examiner further evidence of your knowledge, understanding and business orientation.

All variances could arise from setting poor standards, but they could also be caused by specific factors. For example, the adverse materials variance could have arisen from a combination of a price and usage variance. An adverse materials price variance shows that you have paid more for your materials that you expected. This could have arisen from:

- paying more for your materials: this could be caused by increased market prices, using different suppliers (perhaps they have shorter lead times which enable you to carry less stock), or buying better quality materials
- using different materials: you could have changed the specification, product mix, or used better quality materials that cost more than you planned.

An adverse materials usage variance arises from using more material than was expected. This could have been caused by:

- production inefficiencies: the company could have an increased scrap rate because of poor quality materials, machinery difficulties, or untrained staff
- using different materials: a changed specification or product mix.

While I have talked about both materials variances being adverse, the total adverse variance could be a combination of one adverse variance and a favourable one. The same is true of the favourable labour variance.

Possible explanations for a favourable labour rate variance would include:

- paying less for staff than was expected, perhaps the wages settlement was lower than budgeted
- using different staff than budgeted: perhaps the process has been simplified and less skilled staff can now be used.

Possible explanations for a favourable labour efficiency variance could include:

- improved productivity: this could arise from method or process improvements, or improved morale
- using different staff than were budgeted for.

While some fixed cost variances can also be traced to price and usage, they can also be caused by:

- An increase in the activity level. Fixed costs are not totally fixed; they are fixed within certain levels of activity – moving up in 'steps' as the business reaches its maximum capacity. The fixed costs would also have been budgeted to reflect the activity level, and a significant increase might lead to increases in fixed overheads. For example, the 20 per cent increase in activity might have required additional staff. These staff would have had to have been recruited and trained, giving an adverse variance in the HR budget.
- Timing errors: the organisation might have budgeted to run a training programme in March, but it was brought forward to January. This would show an adverse variance on January's budget and a favourable variance in March.

Now you have the opportunity to finish by reinforcing your business orientation.

To understand the business's performance in the period you need to both analyse these variances and discover why there was an increase in the activity level. It is possible that the increase was unexpected, possibly as a result of bad planning, and the unexpected increase in activity might be pressurising both the management and systems.

If you feel you would like some more help with this question you should read Chapters 11 and 15 in Davies (1999), or alternatively you could try Chapters 15 and 16 in Dyson (2000b).

May 2004 MI exam: Section A finance question

Optional question 2

Your organisation is reviewing its capital budgeting programme. The finance department has just sent the HR manager the following figures on a project proposal that she has put forward, with the attached note.

Note from Finance:
Have just done a run through your project using a couple of quick approaches. It looks viable. We may have to do some more elaborate calculations for the board, if there is a lot of competition for the capital budget next year.

Assumed project cost and income:

	£000	£000
Total cost of project		600
Expected net cash flow		
Year		
1	24	
2	60	
3	120	
4	240	
5	360	
6	55	*859*
Net Return		259

(i) Payback method calculation:

Year	Net cash flow £000	Cumulative net cash flow £000
0	− 600	− 600
1	24	− 576
2	60	− 516
3	120	− 396
4	240	− 156
5	360	204
6	55	259

(ii) Discounted payback calculation

Year	Net cash flow £000	Discount factors	Present value at 9% £000	Cumulative present value £000
0	– 600	1.000	– 600	– 600
1	24	0.9174	22	– 578
2	60	0.8417	51	– 527
3	120	0.7722	93	– 435
4	240	0.7084	170	– 265
5	360	0.6499	234	– 31
6	55	0.5963	33	2

Your manager has asked you to interpret the figures and explain the note. (You must assume that she has a limited knowledge of financial matters.)

Now let us think about what this question is testing. It is really testing your understanding of two project appraisal methods.

First, it is asking you to explain payback and the net present value methods to your manager. This is an opportunity to show your knowledge, and to tackle this question you have to understand the principles underlying both payback and net present value. It is also an opportunity to illustrate your presentation skills, as you have to explain these to your manager who has 'limited knowledge of financial matters'.

Second, it is also asking you to interpret the figures. This gives you the opportunity to show your understanding of other investment appraisal techniques and sensitivity analysis.

Evidence of knowledge

You should know enough about investment appraisal, payback and net present value to show evidence of your knowledge about payback and a little business orientation.

The first table shows that your project has an initial cost of £600,000 with benefits (probably cost reduction) of £859,000 over the following six years. It shows that over six years the project will improve profitability by £259,000, with the bulk of the benefits (£720,000) occurring in years 3–5. As both the costs and benefits are assumed, you ought to check that they are realistic, as they underpin the methods Finance has used to assess the project's viability. You will have to disclose the underlying assumptions, and it might also be useful to prepare a pessimistic view of the project's benefits. This is particularly important as most of the benefits arise in the third to fifth years, and their timing makes it more difficult to predict theses accurately.

As the company would be investing £600,000, the Finance department is concerned with how long it takes the project to repay the initial investment. This is measured in the second table, the payback method, which shows that the benefits repay the original investment during the fifth year.

The sooner the company gets its original investment back the better, as:

- It is more certain – a lot of things could happen between now and the start of the third year when the significant benefits start.
- The company can reinvest the money elsewhere in the business.
- Even with low inflation, the £55,000 received by the end of the sixth year will not be worth as much as £55,000 at the end of the first year.

The next step is the difficult task of explaining net present value to someone with 'a limited knowledge of financial matters'. Now show evidence of your knowledge of net present value and your communication skills.

The third table looks at net present value. Net present value (NPV) is an investment appraisal technique that takes account of the 'time value of money'. What does this mean? If interest rates are 10 per cent, £91 received today is worth the same as £100 received next year. Or alternatively £100 received today is worth more than £100 received tomorrow, because you can invest it and earn compound interest. Compound interest tells you how much you will receive in a year's time if you invest today at a given interest rate. NPV flips the coin, and looks at the investment from the opposite perspective.

NPV is based on the concept of present value. *Present value* tells you how much money you would have to invest today to receive certain cash flows in the future, at a given interest rate. So if interest rates are 10 per cent, the present value of £100 received next year is £91. This present value is then compared with the amount you are being asked to invest, with the difference between the two being the net present value. So if you were only being asked to invest £85, the net present value would be £6 (*the present value of £91 less the £85 you are asked to invest*). An investment showing a positive net present value is earning more than the chosen interest rate, whereas an investment with a negative net present value is earning less.

To calculate the present value, and consequently the net present value, I am *discounting* future cash by 10 per cent. Different businesses use different discount rates, and deciding on the discount rate is often seen as subjective. (I have picked 10 per cent to explain net present value because it is possible to work the arithmetic out without a calculator.) The discount rate has to reflect the opportunity cost (interest rates), inflation, and the risk involved in the investment. The Finance department, like that of most commercial companies, has used the weighted average cost of capital (WACC) as the discount rate, as the return from all investments should be greater than their funding cost. No one would borrow money at 9 per cent and invest in something only earning 6 per cent! As the cost of capital is being used as the discount rate, a positive net present value shows that the investment has a greater return than the cost of funding it.

Now I have explained the principles of net present value, let me explain the third table that applies this to your project.

You will see that the project's cost is shown as occurring in 'Year 0'. That is just the accountant's way of expressing today. If you look at the column marked 'discount rate' you will see it says 1 in year 0, as £1 received today is worth £1.00. Now look at the next row, for year 1. Here you will see that £1 received at the end of the first year is only worth 91.74 pence when discounted at 9 per cent. The next column multiplies the net cash by the discount rate, so the £24,000 cash received at the end of the first year has a present value of £22,000. The final column shows the cumulative present value, and if you look at the sixth year you will find that your project has a net present value of 2. This means that, if interest rates were 9 per cent, we would normally be asked to invest £602,000 to get these returns. We are only being asked to invest £600,000, so the investment' is viable – but only just.

And finally some further evidence of your understanding and your business orientation.

While net present value takes account of the 'time value of money', it is totally dependent on the information in the project brief. If we do not get £10,000 of the savings expected in year 5 the project would not be viable, as we would have a negative net present value of £4,499 (*I have calculated this by deducting the current NPV of £2,000 from £10,000 x the fifth year's discount factor of 0.6499 – £6,499. 10,000 is always an easy number to use!*).

The current financial analysis shows that the project is viable and takes five years to repay the original cost, and has a small net present value when discounted at 9 per cent. If there is capital rationing and the project is compared with others, its low net present value would probably lead to its rejection. If finance used another tool, the internal rate of return, it would probably be the same as our cost of capital – 9 per cent. However, this is an HR project and there may be social benefits that could also be quantified, using a 'cost–benefit' approach. Consequently before we do any further financial analysis, I recommend that we need to check our underlying assumptions to ensure that all the benefits have been costed and that they are realistic and achievable.

If you feel you would like some more help with this question you should read Chapter 16 in Davies (1999), or you could try Chapter 19 in Dyson (2003).

November 2003 and May 2004 MI exams: Section B finance questions

We think this is the hardest section in the exam paper, as you have to answer seven questions and you only really have around eight minutes to answer each question. However you can use diagrams, flow charts, bullet points and so on, as long as you give a 'coherent explanation'. We think you would have to use these to answer the finance questions well in the available time. Diagrams are particularly useful, as you can explain a lot in a little time, and do not be afraid to use the equivalent of text boxes to reinforce your main points.

Always take every opportunity to relate the questions to your organisation. It will make answering them easier (after all, you know about your organisation and its financial practices), but it will also be evidence of your business orientation and application ability.

There are three finance questions in both the exam papers. The November 2003 paper asks questions about:

- the information that can be gained from balance sheets

- the difference between profitability and liquidity

- investment appraisal techniques.

The May 2004 paper asks questions about:

- using marginal costing when you have a limiting factor

- standard costing and variance analysis

- the ratios found in a set of published accounts.

Let us look at the three finance questions and consider:

- what they are testing

- what you should know

- how you could present the information in the available time to earn the maximum marks.

November 2003 examination

First question

6. Write a short article for the organisational newsletter on the nature and value of the information that can be gained from balance sheets. Illustrate your answer with reference to your own organisation.

Now let us start by thinking about what this question is testing.

First, it is asking you to write 'a short article for the organisational newsletter'. This gives you an opportunity to show your presentation skills. The article has to be clear and written for people who have little or no financial knowledge.

Second, it is asking you to explain what a balance sheet is, and why it is useful. This gives you the opportunity to show your knowledge and understanding.

Third, it is asking you to 'illustrate your answer with reference to your own organisation'. The examiner is trying to test your application capability. You should have looked at your own organisation's balance sheet, and are being offered the opportunity to use it to answer the question.

The question clearly tells you your audience, which determines your style, and it asks you to explain the balance sheet in your organisation. You should already know what a balance sheet is, what your organisation's balance sheet looks like, and what it tells you about your organisation.

This is not designed to be a 'model answer', and is based on a commercial organisation. However a good answer should include evidence of your presentation skills and knowledge about your balance sheet.

> The balance sheet is a 'snapshot' of our business on a certain day, showing what our business has, and what it owes. Like any photo, it can be taken from a number of different perspectives and ours looks at our business from the investors' point of view. It shows what the business has, its assets, and deducts what it owes, its liabilities. It finishes with the shareholders' investment in the business.
>
> The assets are grouped into:
>
> • our long-term assets that we intend to keep and use for more than a year (called our fixed assets)
>
> • those we can realise in the short term (our current assets).
>
> Our liabilities, referred to as our 'creditors', are classified in the same way.
>
> The balance sheet deducts our liabilities from our assets in two stages, as you will see in the model below.

Fixed assets

- Our offices, computers and cars which are called *tangible assets*

Current assets

- Our stocks, debtors and cash

−

Creditors due in a year

- This includes our short term loans, the money we owe suppliers, and the government

*These are deducted from our current assets, to show a sub total called the **net current assets**. This is then added to the fixed assets to give another sub total called the **total assets less current liabilities***

=

Net current assets

Total assets less current liabilities
Our fixed assets + net current assets

−

Creditors due in more than a year

- Our long term loans

*These are now deducted to show our **net assets**. You'll see this is the same number as the total of our capital and reserves*

Net assets

Capital and reserves

- This is the cash the shareholders have invested in our business + all of the profits retained in the business to fund its growth since it started in 1984

You will find two balance sheets, one for this year and one for last year, so that you can see how the value of our business has changed since last year.

Now you have shown the examiner you know what the balance sheet is, and what it looks like, you can now show the examiner you understand why it is useful, and that you know some of the relevant ratios.

The balance sheet is an important document as it shows you whether we can pay our bills when they fall due – our business's financial health. You have heard of businesses that close because they cannot pay their suppliers, or have borrowed too much money from the bank. Fortunately we are not in that position!

If you look at our balance sheet you will find that we have £1.47 in current assets for every £1.00 we have to repay next year (a ratio called the 'current ratio'). As we manage to turn our materials back into cash fairly quickly, this means that we should not have any difficulty paying suppliers. We have used cheap loans to help finance our business, and are borrowing 60p for every £1.00 the shareholders have invested or retained in the business. (This is reflected in a ratio called the 'debt to equity ratio'. It is expressed in a different way as '60 per cent', as our loans are 60 per cent of the shareholders' investment.)

If you feel you would like some more help with this question you should read Chapter 4 in Davies (1999) or you could try Chapter 6 in Dyson (2003).

Second question

7. The Chief Executive Officer has just announced a series of cost cutting initiatives, due to liquidity problems. Since he has assured the staff on many occasions that the company is very profitable, they do not understand his cause for concern. Write explanatory notes on this in preparation for a staff briefing session.

Now let us start by thinking about what this question is testing. First, it is asking you to write 'explanatory notes' for a 'staff briefing session'. This means that your presentation style will be very different from the last question. It will be in note form, but has to illustrate your communication and persuasion skills.

Second, it is asking you to explain the difference between profitability and liquidity. This gives you the opportunity to show your knowledge and understanding, and put it into a commercial context. This will show both your business orientation and your application capability.

You should know the main reasons why profit differs from cash:

- the profit and loss account ignores when the cash is received from customers, and when suppliers are paid

- three of the accounting adjustments are not cash-related

- only a proportion of capital expenditure, this year's use of the asset reflected in the depreciation charge, is charged to the profit and loss account

- acquisitions, disposals and loan repayments do not show on the profit and loss account.

Now let us look at how you could present the information in the time available: This is not designed to be a 'model answer'. However a good answer should include similar features.

First, set the scene:

> *Staff briefing notes.*
> *1. Explain the difference between profit and cash by asking a series of questions:*
> - We have discussed our business's profitability, so I would like to ask you a question:
>   Q: 'If I buy a pen for £5 and sell it for £10, how much profit do I make?'
>   A: '£5, and a good profit margin'
>   Q: 'Imagine I pay £5 cash today to buy the pen, and give my customers a month to pay me – How much cash do I have in my pocket today?'
>   A: Minus £5. But the profit on the pen is the same whether I am paid or not.

Now show further evidence of your knowledge and understanding.

2. Explain the profit and loss account:
- It looks at the products we have shipped to our customers and deducts the costs that relate to those sales, not the cash coming in and going out.
- This means that a profitable business is selling its goods for more than it costs to deliver them to its customers.
- Profit doesn't tell you anything about a business's cash position. Profitable businesses can go bust!

3. Explain the cash flow statement.
Other things affect cash including:
- when our customers pay, and when we pay our suppliers
- how much stock we have to finance
- our interest and tax bills
- our capital expenditure
- whether we are buying, or selling, businesses
- the dividends paid to investors.

This is in another financial statement – the *cash flow* statement. It looks at the last period and shows:
- where the cash came from
- where it was spent
- whether we are living within our means
- whether we needed additional finance to fund our business.

4. The borrowing option.
Ask them to think about their debt – you:
- try to live within your means
- do not want to borrow so much that all your salary is going to pay interest
- cut back if you are overspending.

Explain it is the same for businesses:
- The recent expansion programme improved our profits, but has left us short of cash (accountants refer to this as 'liquidity problems').
- It makes sense to start to look at cutting our costs, so we can keep comfortably within our borrowing limits.
- It is not sensible to increase our debt (accountants call this our gearing).

If you feel you would like some more help with this question you should read: Chapter 5 in Davies (1999) or you could try Chapter 4 in Dyson (2003).

Third question

    8. You have shortly to sit on a committee which has been formed to advise management on which capital projects should be chosen for the coming financial year. How would you prepare for this meeting? Test yourself by writing explanatory notes on two possible approaches to making these choices.

Now let us start by thinking about what this question is testing. First, you have to describe how you would prepare for the meeting. In outlining your preparation you have the opportunity to show the examiner your business orientation and summarise your knowledge of all investment appraisal techniques and their limitations.

    You then have to explain two possible approaches to appraising capital projects. This gives you the opportunity to show your detailed knowledge and understanding of two of the techniques. We shall be illustrating the accounting rate of return, which your organisation may call the average return on capital employed, and cost–benefit analysis. While these are probably the least popular appraisal methods, we illustrated net present value and payback in the alternative question in Section A of the May 2004 exam paper (see page 87).

    You should know the main things to consider when you are evaluating projects, and have a good understanding of all of the project appraisal techniques (after all, they are frequently tested in the exam). Let us look at how you could present this information to your best advantage in the time available.

    This is not designed to be a 'model answer'. However a good answer should include these components.

    The first part of the question is a summary of your meeting preparation, and this gives you the opportunity to show the examiner evidence of your knowledge of the project appraisal process, and the general limitations of the financial project evaluation process.

Meeting preparation
Initially: revise the four main methods for assessing projects:
- payback
- accounting rate of return
- discounted cash flow (both net present value and the internal rate of return)
- cost–benefit analysis.

Review the corporate plan, to ascertain the strategic business's direction, and understand the strategic importance of the projects.

As business cases are based on estimated costs and benefits, I would look at each business case to review its underlying assumptions, then see what happens to the project's viability if these were modified (for example if the machine cost 10% more, or the cost savings were 10 % less).

You have now shown the examiner evidence of your business orientation and that you understand that the business case is only as good as its underlying assumptions and the data. Now you have to show the examiner your knowledge of two investment appraisal techniques.

Cost–benefit analysis
Whilst all project appraisal techniques consider the tangible costs and benefits of a project, cost–benefit analysis goes one stage further as it includes social costs and benefits. While it is rarely used in commercial organisations, it is widely used in the public sector where most projects have social as well as financial benefits.

To illustrate this I will consider a project to build additional lanes on a motorway to relieve congestion. Enlarging the motorway would increase the usage (as there is less congestion) and reduce the journey time.

In addition to the obvious construction costs, cost–benefit analysis would also consider environmental costs. The environmental effect of the emissions from the additional journeys would be included in the project's costs.

The benefits of the wider motorway would be:
- shorter journey time

- reduced accidents and fatalities
- lower emissions per journey, as the journey time would be shorter.

These benefits would be quantified and would form part of the project submission. The project evaluation would then apply payback and discounted cash flow techniques to these costs and benefits.

While cost–benefit analysis is the only suitable approach for projects that have largely social benefits, calculating the costs of emissions, the value of shorter journey time, traffic accidents and fatalities is clearly subjective. However, there are computer models widely used in the public sector that do this.

The accounting rate of return

This is a useful tool in the commercial sector where investors want a return on their investment that:
- compensates them for the investment risk
- is greater than the business's cost of capital.

It expresses the average profit as a percentage of the investment's cost. For example:

Our HR department want to buy a new computer system costing £50,000. Over the next five years it will generate annual cost savings of £25,000 a year – £125,000 in total. The total profit in the five years would be £75,000 (*£125,000 – £50,000*), and the average profit £15,000 a year (*£75,000 ÷ 5 years*). The accounting rate of return would be 30 per cent (*£15,000 ÷ £50,000*).

This return is then compared with the business's actual, or target, return on capital employed to assess the viability of the project.

However, the accounting rate of return does not consider the timing of the cash flows. A project would have the same return if it had the same cost, and total benefits, even if £100,000 of the benefits were received in the fifth year. But it would be riskier and have a lower real return.

If you feel you would like some more help with this question you should read Chapter 16 in Davies (1999) or Chapter 19 in Dyson (2003) (this does not cover cost–benefit analysis).

May 2004 examination

First question

> 2. Your organisation has a limited number of skilled workers who are involved in several product lines with different sales values and variable costs. Explain what costing concept you would use to help you decide on the optimum product mix and why. What are the wider implications for your organisation?

Let us start by thinking about what this question is testing. First, it is asking you to explain marginal costing, the costing method that would be used to determine the optimum product mix in this situation. This gives you the opportunity to show your knowledge and understanding.

Second, it is asking you to explain why you would use marginal costing. This gives you an opportunity to show your presentation skills and business orientation.

The final part of the question asks you to consider the 'wider implications for your organisation'. This gives you an opportunity to show your business orientation.

You should know that marginal costing is the only costing concept that can be used to make this type of decision, as it can identify the contribution per labour hour (the limiting factor in this example). We think the easiest way to explain this in the time allowed is with a very simple worked example. If you use examples, make sure that you keep the arithmetic very simple.

Now you know that this is not a 'model answer', but I think you will find that it covers the main points in the time available. First, you have to show the examiner evidence of your knowledge of marginal costing and its appropriateness to this situation.

> The most appropriate costing concept to use is marginal costing, as it does not include allocated fixed costs. Marginal costing analyses costs into those that are:
> - *variable*: they change with the level of volume/activity
> - *fixed*: within certain levels of activity these costs do not change, but after that these costs move up in steps.
>
> Only the variable costs are included in the product cost. These variable costs are deducted from the selling price to give the

product's contribution (or gross profit). As we have a limited number of skilled workers, our profit would be maximised if we produced the products that gave us the best contribution per skilled labour hour. This is illustrated in the example below, where the company makes three products:

	Finest	Standard	Value
Selling price	10.00	8.00	6.00
Variable cost	(6.00)	(5.00)	(3.00)
Gross profit/contribution	4.00	3.00	3.00
Labour hours to make a unit	4.0	2.0	1.5
Contribution per labour hour	1.00	1.50	2.00

> *While Finest has the best unit contribution, it has the worst contribution per labour hour*

The best contributor per labour hour is 'Value'. Consequently, if we wanted to optimise our profitability we would phase our production to satisfy all of the demand for 'Value', then the demand for 'Standard' and finally 'Finest'.

We have used an example, as we think it is the quickest way to explain this application. When using examples, make sure the numbers are simple, and do not use fancy names for your products – A, B and C will do, otherwise you will waste too much time!

Now for your business orientation.

However, this may not be the best *commercial* decision. For example:

- Our marketing strategy could be to develop our sales of 'Finest'.
- Our customers may want to buy the full range of our products.
- We may be unable to produce any 'Finest', leaving the market open to our competitors.

If you feel you would like some more help with this question you should read Chapter 12 in Davies (1999) or Chapter 17 in Dyson (2003).

Second question

5. As part of a development programme one of your staff is to attend a monthly budget review meeting. In preparation for this, explain to him what the different kinds of variances are, the issues surrounding the setting up of standards and the limitations of the process.

Now let us start by thinking about what this question is testing. First you need to remember that you are explaining standard costing and variance analysis to one of your staff on a development programme. This means that he/she is probably relatively unfamiliar with financial jargon, and you will have to communicate simply and effectively.

The question is asking you to explain 'the different kinds of variances'. This is an opportunity to show your knowledge of the different types of variances.

Then it is asking you to discuss 'the issues surrounding the setting up of standards' and the 'limitations of the process'. This allows you to show your knowledge and understanding of the standard costing process.

You should know about standard costing, and how variances can be described as adverse or favourable. You know that direct cost variances can be caused by poor standards, and changes in price, volume, or usage. Now let us look at how you can convey the main points effectively in the time allowed.

This is not designed to be a 'model answer'. However a good answer should include these elements. First, show your knowledge of standard costing and variances.

In most businesses the planned unit, or process cost, is developed using a budgeting tool called *standard costing*. This multiplies the planned costs by the planned usage at the planned level of activity to give the budgeted cost. Both the costs and the planned activity are those that we think we can realistically achieve, although other businesses might use targets. The differences between our budgeted standard cost and the actual costs are called *variances*. Variances either improve the business's profitability (*favourable* variances) or reduce it (*adverse* variances). We show our adverse variances in brackets. We analyse costs into direct costs (product related) and indirect costs (general business expenditure). Direct cost variances occur for one of three reasons – either you are:

- making more, or less, than you expected (a *volume* variance)
- paying more, or less, than you expected (a *price* variance)
- using more, or less, than you planned (a *usage* variance).

However, these terms are not always used. For example, the finance department call our labour variances either *rate* variances (when it cost more because we have paid the staff more) or *efficiency* variances (when it has taken longer to make than we expected). We only analyse these variances, but in other parts of the group they further analyse these into subvariances.

Indirect cost variances can also occur because the expenditure has been wrongly phased, with the actual expenditure occurring in a different month than originally planned.

The advantage of identifying variances is that you can identify *why* the variances have occurred, ask the right question, and take appropriate corrective action.

Now show your business orientation by looking at the information needed and the limitations of a standard costing system.

To develop a standard cost system you need to have detailed information about the cost and quantity of the direct materials, labour, and overheads used in making the product. Standard costing is time consuming and is only as good as the quality of the estimates used to develop the standards. Whilst it helps you trace the cause for the variances, it doesn't actually tell you what has happened.

If you feel you would like some more help with this question you should read Chapter 11 in Davies (1999) or Chapter 16 in Dyson (2003).

Third question

> 6. A colleague has been reading the company accounts. She e-mails 'What are all these ratios about?' With examples, explain to her what information the different kinds of ratios provide and what limitations they have. How would an understanding of ratios be of use in your organisation?

Now let us think about what this question is testing. It is really testing your understanding of the financial ratios shown in company accounts. First it is asking you to explain, using examples, the different kinds of ratios and their limitations, to a colleague. This is an opportunity to show your knowledge, and to tackle this question you will be illustrating your presentation skills, as you have to explain these to your colleague. Do not forget that the question is also asking you to look at the ratios' limitations.

It is also asking you to explain how understanding the ratios would be useful in your organisation. This gives you the opportunity to show your business orientation by quoting some of the ratios from your organisation.

We think this is possibly the most difficult question in the paper, not because of the knowledge you are expected to have, but because of the time you have to communicate it. (In our standard ratio analysis notes there are 32 ratios, as these are the ones clients regularly use!) You cannot show the examiner everything you know in eight minutes, particularly as you also have to discuss their limitations and their usefulness to your organisation! You have to find a way to classify the ratios, and identify:

- the most important ones

- the ones you are likely to find in your organisation's accounts.

We always classify ratios into four groups:

- *Solvency ratios*: the acid test, current ratio, **gearing** and **interest cover**. We might also talk about the working capital ratios here as they affect the acid test and the current ratio.

- *Profitability ratios*: the gross margin, **operating margin** (or **return on sales**), **the return on capital employed** and its subsidiary ratios.

- *Investment ratios*: including **earnings per share, dividend per share**, price earnings, dividend yield, **total shareholder return**, cash flow per share.

- *Productivity ratios*: like sales per employee, profit per employee.

Obviously you will not find all of these in your organisation's accounts (if you are not listed on the stock exchange you will not find any investment ratios), and we have boldfaced the ratios commonly found. Your organisation could show different ratios, as ratios are just a measure of its performance. Consequently different ratios are relevant in different businesses. Your organisation may also define the ratios slightly differently from those found in a textbook (this particularly applies to gearing and return on capital employed).

You have two options for tackling this question. Either you cover ratios in general or you discuss one ratio category in detail. Do not forget that you can show your business orientation by quoting some of the ratios from your company's accounts.

This time we can honestly say that this is not a model answer, as you could not possibly write this in the time available. We want to show how you could give a few general paragraphs and look at either the solvency and profitability ratios. You would only have the time to do one of these in any detail.

First, you have to show the examiner evidence of your knowledge about the ratios you are likely to find in company accounts.

Ratios measure a business's performance, and enable you to benchmark your performance against your competitors. Broadly they can be classified into those measuring our:
- solvency
- profitability
- investment performance
- productivity.

We show a selection of solvency and profitability ratios in our accounts.

Our solvency

Businesses go bust if they can't pay suppliers, or have difficulties with their banks. There are ratios that help measure this.

First, you can see whether we are likely to be able to pay our suppliers, either by working out our creditor days or using a ratio called the current ratio. This tells you how much we have in current assets for every pound we owe:

$$\frac{\text{Current assets}}{\text{Creditors: amounts falling due in a year}}$$

You must look at this ratio in the context of the business, as the size of the current ratio is determined by:
- how long it takes to go through our working capital cycle
- how frequently our customers buy.

You also need to remember that our current ratio has fallen in the last year from 1.61 to 1.47 as we have been:
- trying to become more efficient and reduce our working capital
- reinvesting the cash we have saved in new fixed assets

While this means that we have a lower current ratio, it does not mean that we are insolvent – just more efficient!

If you are concerned about our banking relationships you can look at *gearing* (which tells you how much we have borrowed) and *interest cover* (which tells you if we can afford it). Our measure of gearing is the debt to equity ratio, expressing debt as a percentage of the shareholders' investment in the business:

$$\frac{\text{Total debt}}{\text{Capital and reserves}}$$

Our loans are 60 per cent of the shareholders' equity. Once we know how much we have borrowed, it is important to see if we can afford it. Interest cover shows how many times we can pay the interest from our available profits, and the bigger the number the more affordable our borrowing:

$$\frac{\text{Profit before interest}}{\text{Net interest payable}}$$

We have an interest cover of 10 times, so we should not have any problems with our bank as we can easily pay the interest.

You have seen that most of these ratios are derived from the balance sheet. This means that they are measuring our performance on a particular day, which may not be representative of our position throughout the year.

Our profitability
Everyone is interested in profit. First, we want to know if we are making any profit, and then whether it is enough. If you want to know whether we are selling our products for more than they cost to deliver to our customers you look at the operating profit. The *operating margin* expresses the operating profit as a percentage of our sales:

$$\frac{\text{Operating profit}}{\text{Turnover}}$$

We are making 11 per cent operating margin.

We also show our gross margin, which is the profit after our manufacturing costs (shown as 'cost of sales' on the profit and loss account):

$$\frac{\text{Gross profit}}{\text{Turnover}}$$

Our gross margin is 32 per cent, so this means that 21 per cent of our sales goes to pay for our administration and distribution expenses. This ratio is less useful for benchmarking, as different companies have different definitions of 'cost of sales'.

Then you can look at the profit we are making on the money invested in the business, this is measured by the return on capital employed, which we define as:

$$\frac{\text{Profit before interest and tax}}{\text{Total assets less current liabilities}}$$

This is an important comparative measure as:
- Our return on capital has to be greater than our cost of capital.
- We have one of the highest returns on capital in our sector, 18 per cent, making us attractive for investors.

Now you need to reinforce why you think understanding these ratios would be of benefit to your organisation.

> You can now see that these ratios help us measure and monitor our performance. They help us benchmark ourselves against our competitors, and understand senior managements' decisions. Using these ratios helps us understand that a business needs to be both solvent and profitable if it is to survive.

If you feel you would like some more help with this question you should read Chapter 7 in Davies (1999) or Chapter 9 in Dyson (2003).

SECTION 4

CONCLUSION

5 CONCLUSION

Key points to remember

Time management

- It is critically important to manage your time appropriately in the examination. If you are well prepared and confident as a result, then you will be able to approach the examination tasks calmly and plan the amount of time you are going to spend on each part of the paper and on each question.

- Take time to read through the paper carefully at the outset, think about the questions being asked, and select the ones that you think you can answer fully. Remember that in Section A you can choose as your second question either a finance/accounting question or a statistics question. In Section B there is a reasonable choice of questions from each part of the course. You can therefore be selective and play to your strengths.

- Do not forget that you will normally be expected to include examples from your organisational experience, so knowledge of theory underlying a question may not be sufficient to provide a full answer.

- Do not go on writing beyond the time that you have allocated for the question. This means that you must have decided what the key points you want to make are and that you have gone straight into the question. Do not waste time writing yourself into the question with an irrelevant introduction. Answer the question as directly as you can. Remember that the law of diminishing returns applies here – most of your marks will be gained from the key points that you make, and very little will be achieved by going on beyond this.

- Not completing all questions fully in Section A will most probably lead to a fail grade; not answering seven questions in Section B will most definitely lead to a fail grade.

Planning your answers

- The examiners try to ensure that questions are straightforward and unambiguous and there is not normally the need to 'deconstruct' or interpret the question. However, this does assume that you will be reasonably familiar with the specialised vocabulary of the module and the knowledge indicators. Unfamiliarity can lead to candidates mistakenly interpreting the question and not answering the question as set.

- In answering a question you need to decide what theoretical base you are going to use to analyse, explain or make recommendations about a problem situation. This means you will need to search the knowledge base you have acquired from your study of the module and select appropriate theoretical constructs, principles or methods. These need to be made explicit in your answer. You cannot be given credit for thinking a course idea; it has to be visibly applied, so that your argument or train of thought is transparent.

- Decide on key points that you are going to make and assemble these into a coherent set. Bear in mind that overuse of bullet points may result in a fragmented answer, lacking in coherence.

- Decide on what examples you can use from your own organisational experience or recent cases you may have read about in the literature or journals to illustrate your answer and demonstrate application capability.

Postgraduate level

To ensure that your answers are appropriate to a postgraduate-level qualification, you should aim to demonstrate:

- that you can analyse issues using concepts, theoretical constructs, methods and principles

- critical awareness that theoretical constructs may not necessarily match the complexity of a dynamic problem scenario and that any proposed solution, developed using such constructs, may lead to emergent consequences affecting the sustainability of the solution

- an understanding of the way in which concepts, theories, frameworks and approaches can be used to tackle problems and provide insights on which to base practical actions and recommendations

- the ability to communicate lucidly and succinctly your ideas and analyses to specialist and non-specialist audiences

- evidence of reflective practice, that is, being able to learn by reflecting on one's experience, being aware of other stakeholder perspectives and taking a constructively critical approach to problem solving generally

- evidence that you are up to date with current developments and applications of information technology/systems and financial and statistical approaches in the human resource management area, both in your own organisation and generally, through regular reading of *People Management*, the business press and other relevant management journals.

General points

You should ensure that:

- You read the questions carefully and answer all parts.

- Your answer is a direct and explicit response to the question set. Writing all you know in a descriptive and anecdotal way about some topic, hoping that some part will 'hit the target' is unlikely to be awarded a pass grade.

- Your answer is in the format asked for in the question rubric (for example, if a report is asked for, then your answer should be in report format).

- Your use of the course concepts is explicit. You must display your knowledge rather than using it implicitly as you would in a report in your organisation.

- Diagrams and graphical material are clearly laid out and presented, so that they are intelligible, otherwise there is no point in drawing them.

- You use diagrams and text in an interrelated way, that is, do not draw a diagram and then waste time repeating all the information in the diagram as text. A diagram should be accompanied only by a brief textual commentary on salient features.

- You write as legibly as you can. If your writing is hard to read the chances of the examiner misunderstanding what you are trying to say are much greater. If you think that your handwriting is difficult to read, write on alternate lines. Since most people are using word processors these days and are not in the habit of writing for long periods by hand, it is sensible to practise writing examination questions by hand, well in advance of the examination.

- You get plenty of practice doing outline structures for examination questions and writing out some of the answers in full.

- All your work is written in ink, that is, not pencil.

A final word

You should be aware that the examiner and markers generally have a very supportive approach, trying to find ways of giving marks for what is known, rather than trying to deduct marks for any minor errors or omissions. Provided that in your answers you can demonstrate that you have made a serious study of the module and assimilated a reasonable number of the key ideas and concepts, then you should have no difficulty in achieving a pass grade.

REFERENCES

Alter, S. (1997) *Information systems: a management perspective*, Menlo Park, Calif.: Benjamin/Cummings.

Bee, R. and Bee, F. (1999) *Managing information and statistics*, London: CIPD.

Checkland, P.B. and Holwell, S. (1997) *Information, systems and information systems: making sense of the field*. Chichester: Wiley.

Checkland, P.B. and Scholes, J. (1990) *Soft systems metholodogy in action*. Chichester: Wiley.

Davies, D. (1999) *Managing financial information*, London: CIPD.

Dyson, J.R. (2003) *Accounting for non-accounting students*, Harlow: FT Prentice Hall.

Elliot, G. (2004) *Global business information technology: an integrated systems approach.* Addison Wesley.

Mason, R.O. and Mitroff, I.I. (1981) *Challenging strategic planning assumptions: theory, cases and techniques.* Chichester: Wiley.

Rittel, H. (1972) On the planning crisis: systems analysis of the first and second generations. *Bedriftsokonomen*, No. 8, pp. 390–6.

Weaver, P., Lambrou, N. and Walkley, M. (2002) *Practical business systems development using SSADM,* 3rd edn, Harlow: FT Prentice Hall.

INDEX

NOTES